A Dream Fulfilled...

Farm Neck Golf Club

by Charles H. Harff

FIRST EDITION 2004

Book design by Michael Stakem

ISBN: 0-9759437-0-7

In Dedication...

This book is dedicated to my wife, Marion, whose unwavering interest in preserving the ambience and beauty of Martha's Vineyard and whose unstinting encouragement and support both of the efforts involved in the creation and development of Farm Neck and in the writing of this book have played a vital role.

I greatly appreciate her support as well as the support of our three children – Pamela, Blair and Todd – for all too often time demands of the creation and development of Farm Neck, when added to the hours committed to my working career, clearly constrained significantly family time to which we all looked forward.

Beneficiary...

Any net proceeds from the sale of this book will be contributed to the Farm Neck Foundation.

Table of Contents

Aerial view (about 1965) of Farm Neck area and Sengekontacket Pond before development. House in foreground was at Major's Cove with Island Country Club at upper right and Oak Bluffs in the background.

Preface

As Farm Neck's 25th Anniversary approached, it occurred to me that the history of its evolution from a dream to fulfillment should be preserved for a couple of reasons. First and foremost, it is a unique story – probably the only golf course built on a shoestring, and yet of championship caliber. Moreover, Farm Neck was created not as a commercial venture, but as a vital component of preserving a large tract of land which otherwise was destined for extensive development.

Many of those who today so much enjoy and appreciate Farm Neck look at it as one of the finest golf courses in New England, yet they do not know how it came about. Nor do they recognize that the beauty surrounding Farm Neck came perilously close to being significantly eroded by over development. It is both for those who do not know the history of Farm Neck and for those who participated in its origins that this book has been written.

Second, and perhaps without too much modesty, Farm Neck represents the single-most satisfying achievement that Bob Fullem and I have had in our careers. Bob and I first met when we entered the Freshman class at Colgate University in 1947. We became life-long friends as together we went through four years at Colgate and three years at Harvard Law School. Each of us began our legal careers with Wall Street firms, Bob eventually becoming the Senior Partner at Dewey, Ballantine and I becoming the Senior Partner at Chadbourne & Parke. During our careers as Wall Street lawyers we each concentrated on corporate law, specializing in corporate finance, mergers and acquisitions. We were involved in a number of major corporate transactions, including highly contested transactions well publicized in the financial press. Multimillion dollar transactions were more the norm than the exception. Yet as exciting and interesting as our daily work was for each of us, we both readily agree we derived the most satisfaction from our efforts to create what became known as Farm Neck. With the perspective of time, we also believe that Farm Neck constitutes a more meaningful and lasting contribution than the numerous transactions in which we guided our clients. The over 500 acres of beautiful property on Martha's Vineyard will be there, we would hope and expect, for many generations to enjoy, while in many cases the impact of even major corporate transactions have become with hindsight ephemeral at best.

In a sense, the story of the creation and development of Farm Neck is one of vision, hope, and fortunate timing motivated not by individual potential economic gain but by a shared commitment to land preservation, sound environmental management, and a passion to do the very best to make a shared vision a reality. While Bob and I had key roles in this venture, there is no question as you will see as you read further that success depended on many, many others. It clearly needed the financial support of the initial investors in Farm Neck. The early advice and contributions of Doug Mabee, Tim Sweet, John McGrath, Pat Mulligan and Rob Kendall were vital. Without Tim, who worked with us from the very beginning and who has served as the General Manager for 25 years, Farm Neck would not be what it is today.

One: *A BIT OF HISTORY*

Perhaps nothing describes the genesis of Farm Neck better than to say it was created as a labor of love, a vision fulfilled with hard work, perseverance and a good deal of luck. To understand how Farm Neck began and how far it has come, a bit of background history is required.

What is now Farm Neck was once part of the Love and Luce family homesteads established in the 1700's and farmed for a long time with sheep and cattle, as well as agricultural plantings. That area in early deeds was identified as "Farm Neck," with the work "neck" meaning peninsula. The Farm Neck area is rich in history, containing Pulpit Rock, the boulder from which May Lew preached Christianity to the Indians encamped along the shore of Sengekontacket Pond, as well as one of the Island's oldest cemeteries. In the 1700's Farm Neck was an isolated farming community. Not until the coming of the railroad in the twentieth century, which linked Cottage City (now Oak Bluffs) with Edgartown and Vineyard Haven, was the Beach Road developed and more ready access to Farm Neck provided.

Farm Neck also encompassed what later became the Island Country Club, the Island's only 18-hole golf course until it was subsumed into Farm Neck. While that course had many devoted supporters, it was neither irrigated nor of championship caliber. Of course it had the advantage for mid-summer golfers that balls would roll forever on the baked fairways that were almost like concrete when rain was at a premium. While the founders initially named the golf course to be completed in 1979 "The Links at Martha's Vineyard," largely because the back nine was to be designed as a Scottish links type course, the clear history of the area soon prevailed and by the time the course opened it was christened "Farm Neck."

The Strock Purchases & Development

Two brothers, Moses and Alvin Strock, bought the Love and Luce Farms and the Island Country Club as well as a number of other significant properties on Martha's Vineyard over a number of years in the 1950's and 1960's. All in all the Strocks acquired over 2,000 acres with the initial intent of conserving a good bit of the Island's land. Both Moses and Alvin were successful dentists practicing in the Boston area. Each was singularly devoted to Martha's Vineyard and to conserving its open lands as much as possible. The Spring-Summer 1969 edition of *House Beautiful's Vacation Homes* reported:

—————————————————

"When doctors Alvin and Moses Strock and their families began spending their summers on Martha's Vineyard years ago, it presented unsullied vistas of rolling farm land and sandy beaches dotted with quaint villages that recalled the days of whaling ships. To be sure, it was even then a prime vacation area with a few well-developed summer colonies but it was largely untouched by the commercial blight and crowded conditions that mar so many seaside resorts. Then, as the post-war years brought population growth and increased demand for vacation housing, the two brothers began to fear that the Island and its beauty would fall prey to the haphazard development that has destroyed great sections of nearby Cape Cod. They determined to do something about it.

Their aim was not to stop development but to promote it in ways that would preserve as much open space as possible. To this end, with a nephew, Dr. Peter Strock, they formed Island Properties, Inc., and began acquiring land in various parts of the Vineyard."

———————————————

Thus in 1967, Island Properties began with a development of some 60 acres named Waterview Farm on Sengekontacket Pond, off County Road, with 58 house sites, generally about one-half acre or larger, clustered around two open meadows affording virtually all the parcels substantial views of the Pond. Island Properties' sales brochures noted:

———————————————

"Waterview Farm is an approach to the preservation of open land on Martha's Vineyard. By offering a limited number of homesites bounded by many acres of land deeded as conservation areas — Waterview Farm accommodates the natural growth of the Island while preserving large open spaces as natural wildlife habitats and other conservation uses."

———————————————

The Strocks had the foresight to require each of the houses be built of comparable design and materials, with the thought that once fully developed Waterview Farm would be similar in character to the fishing village of Menemsha. The open meadows and the waterfront property continued in Strock ownership for several years. Eventually Bob Fullem and I (we had built summer homes at Waterview Farm in 1970 and 1969, respectively) organized the Waterview Homeowners' Association and worked with the Strocks to transfer title to those properties to the Association.

In March 1970, Moses Strock died and the Strock interests were transferred to Strock Enterprises. Marcus Strock, Moses' son, joined Alvin Strock as general partners of Strock Enterprises with other family members becoming limited partners. The financial burdens of continuing to hold much of the properties consistent with the original conservation intent were compounded by the estate taxes attributable to the Moses Strock estate.

By the early 1970's, the Strock Enterprises planned much greater development than the initial conservation-oriented approach had contemplated. While the Waterview Farm project was relatively modest in scale, they now proposed much more extensive development of their properties abutting Sengekontacket Pond that included the two farm properties and the Island Country Club. Their proposal included the design and building of a new 18-hole golf course on which the new lots, generally only one-quarter acre in size, would abut the fairways of the new course. They also contemplated comparable density development of the remaining property between Waterview Farm and the Fresh Pond area to the South (the other side of Fresh Pond was later developed by others as "Sengekontacket"), as well as the Major's Cove abutting the Felix Neck Wildlife Sanctuary. The magnitude of the Strock's proposal soon encountered opposition from a number of people interested in maintaining the open character of the beautiful properties abutting Sengekontacket Pond. Among the opponents were several Harthaven residents and Bob Fullem and I.

Establishing the Martha's Vineyard Commission

In August 1973 a bill was introduced in the Massachusetts legislature proposing the establishment of the Martha's Vineyard Commission, a proposal intended to protect land and water on Martha's Vineyard. As noted by the Supreme Judicial Court of Massachusetts in its opinion of March 23, 1977:

———————————————

"The legislation was intended to respond (as the General Court could believe) to the threat of destruction of the ecological and other special values of the Island through steeply increasing commercial development of its land and water resources which would not be adequately contained or regulated merely by action that could or would be initiated by the individual towns."[1]

———————————————

Probably not coincidentally, on October 25, 1973, almost immediately following the introduction of the proposed legislation intended to establish the Martha's Vineyard Commission, Island Properties filed a preliminary sub-division plan with the Oak Bluffs Planning Board. That plan contemplated some 824 building lots on 507 acres. It met the town by-law which permitted minimum lot sizes of 10,000 square feet (1/4 acre). Island Properties filed definitive plans with the Oak Bluffs Planning Board on April 12, 1974, and these plans were approved by the Planning Board on June 7, 1974. Interestingly, nearly a month before Island Properties filed its definitive plans, under the sponsorship of the governor of Massachusetts, further efforts to enact legislation establishing the Martha's Vineyard Commission was introduced. This legislation was approved on July 27, 1974 and enacted as an emergency law effective immediately "to prevent irreversible damage to the Island and ultimately to its economy."[2]

In the legislation establishing the Martha's Vineyard Commission, the Commission was required within a year to set standards and criteria for determining whether proposed developments on Martha's Vineyard would have the potential of having regional impact or critical planning concern and to designate areas that would meet those criteria. Pending this determination, a moratorium was imposed on town authorities for granting of permits on developments of any significant scale. Once the Commission established the criteria under which it would act, it was open to consider nominations of areas that should be designated by it as having regional impact or critical planning concern.

One of the first nominations to the Martha's Vineyard Commission was filed in February 1976 by Pare Lorentz, a resident of Harthaven, appearing on behalf of himself and a number of others, to designate the Strock properties along Sengekontacket as a district of critical planning concern. That petition noted:

"The vital role the areas presently under consideration play in the ecology of the Island has been recognized by Dr.

Strock, a principal in the ownership of the lands, in a letter he wrote on October 25, 1973, to the Oak Bluffs Planning Board, a copy of which is in the Commission's file:

> *'Thus, the applicant naturally agrees with the Town's concern for its future and the important role that these properties will play in that future from an ecological, sociological, and financial point of view. Thus, the applicant looks forward to discussing with the Planning Board, other town agencies, and all citizens of Oak Bluffs, the importance of proper planned use of the subject properties, as this use relates to:*
> > *...Water Quality in Sengekontacket and Wigglesworth Ponds*
> > *...Sanitary Sewerage*
> > *...Water Supply*
> > *...Soil Erosion*
> > *...Wet Lands...'."*

In the conclusion of the petition, it stated:

"The issue presently before the Commission is not whether or not considerable planning has been done by the developer with regard to Waterview III, IV and V. The real issue is whether or not the land here involved, because of its special characteristics, should be designated a district of critical planning concern. The first section of c. 637 [the Act establishing the Commission] makes this indelibly clear:

'SECTION L. Whereas, it is hereby declared that:
...(c) the protection of the health, safety, and general welfare of Island residents and visitors requires the establishment of a regional commission whose purpose shall be to ensure that henceforth the land usages which will be permitted are those which will not be unduly detrimental to those values or to the economy of the Island;
...(d) the preserving and enhancing of these values <u>*requires*</u> *the designation of districts of critical planning concern and the recognition of developments of regional impact, and the review thereof by the regional commission;...' (Emphasis supplied).*

The duty of the Martha's Vineyard Commission is directed to the land, not to the developers of it. The developer here would have the Commission decline jurisdiction here because of the extent of planning and covenants the developer has already undertaken for the 800 lots involved. The irony of this approach is obvious: the amount of planning by the developer to date only serves to underscore the critical nature of the present parcels."[3]

On March 4, 1976, the Martha's Vineyard Commission designated the Strock properties abutting Sengekontacket Pond as a district of critical planning concern. The Commission, in explaining its designation stated:

"Information available to the Commission supports a finding that the Pond District is of regional importance, that there exist problems of uncontrolled or inappropriate development within the district, and affecting areas outside the district, indeed the entire Island, and that there are advantages to be gained by development of the area in a controlled manner. The Commission specifically finds that controlled development of lands and waters within the Pond District is essential to the prevention of pollution of ground and surface waters, the protection of water quality, and to preserving an adequate water supply. In addition, lands and waters within the Pond District contain, support and affect important wildlife habitats. They are essential to marine and shell fishing within and affected by activities in the District, each of which is vital to the Island's economy. Traffic generated by development within this District will adversely affect the safety and welfare of Island residents and visitors. Development will probably overburden the

ability of the Town to supply essential public services to present and future residents. Furthermore, this area contributes substantially to the Island's unique cultural, historic, and economic values. This area offers irreplaceable recreational opportunities. As fragile resources, lands and waters within the District are extremely sensitive to pollution, and the destruction of irreplaceable resources.

The Commission finds that development within the District must be controlled to prevent harm to the public health, safety, and general welfare of persons who might undertake such development and to present and future Island residents and visitors.

In considering the problems of inappropriate or uncontrolled development within the Pond District, the Commission finds *that so fragile are these lands and waters and the values they create and support that to maintain and enhance the health, safety and general welfare of Island residents and visitors, and for present and future generations, special development controls within the District must be adopted.*

In considering the advantages to be gained by development in a controlled manner, the Commission finds that development which conforms to regulations to be established pursuant to the guidelines adopted by this Decision will contribute much to solving the problems of uncontrolled or inappropriate development." [4]

———————————

The Commission also determined that development in a district of critical planning concern would require average density not exceeding 1-1/2 acres for each dwelling unit and proposed to limit development to no more than 1/20th of the permitted housing units each year.

THE GRAPEVINE, a Martha's Vineyard weekly newspaper, reported in its March 10, 1976 edition that:

———————————

"By a vote of 11 to 2, with 2 abstaining, the Martha's Vineyard Commission voted Thursday night to designate the consolidated nominations of the Island Properties Etc. and Major's Cove in Oak Bluffs, but not in Edgartown, as a district of critical planning concern. Among the suggested guidelines are a 1/20th growth rate, a minimum lot size of 60,000 square feet (1-1/2 acres)...".

———————————

The article also reported:

———————————————————

"In discussing the planned subdivision by Dr. Alvin Strock, George Mathiesen pointed out that the number of building permits issued in Oak Bluffs has been holding steady at about 40 houses a year. The proposed growth rate of 1/10th would allow Strock to build 80 houses a year, which would double the town growth rate if no other building permits are granted.

Edith Potter said that despite Dr. Strock's claims, there would be an immense impact on Martha's Vineyard if the proposed development were allowed. She then offered an amendment that halved the growth rate to 1/20th a year.

The Grapevine asked MVC attorney Donald Connors why he believes that the MVC has jurisdiction over Strock subdivisions that had been registered before the effective date of Chapter 637, which created the MVC. Objections had been raised that this interpretation does away with the grandfather clause that protects existing projects and works from new legislation. Connors said that he was reluctant to discuss the matter freely because there had been a hint of court action at the meeting. Richard Thorman, Strock's representative, warned that the MVC was pushing 'this thing into an area Connors appreciates.' Thorman was later asked directly if he or Strock were planning legal action against the MVC and he said only that they have good legal advisors but that his remarks at the hearing could not be directly interpreted as a threat of legal action.

Connors told the Grapevine that he had informed the MVC that one of the major legal issues involved in the regulatory scheme set up by Chapter 637 is whether or not they have the authority to regulate land use when a person has definitive plan approval under the zoning law.

'On the face of the act, there is no specific exemption for plans having such approval or for land shown on plans. It's a serious legal question but it appears on the face of the act that there is such authority in the MVC.'"

———————————

In the March 12, 1976 edition of the *Vineyard Gazette*, in an editorial entitled "Called to Action," Henry Beetle Hough, its editor, stated:

———————————

"In its decision on the project of Island Properties Inc. for development of historic Farm Neck and the slopes of Sengekontacket Pond, the Martha's Vineyard commission has lived up to its responsibilities in an encouraging and clear-cut fashion. The wounded outcry and implied threats of the Strock interests are hardly justified, however, when it is considered that the Commission's limit of one house to each acre and a half is precisely what the present zoning regulations of the town of Oak Bluffs require in that area. Should a new plan come before the town zoning board, this is the limit that could be allowed.

It must be realized that further plans of this same developer, extending its borders around the Dodger's Hole, bring the contemplated number of house sites to more than 1,400. No provision of open space or plan could offset the sheer impact of even 800 new houses, now and in the next few years, on the Island as a whole."

Challenge to the Commission

Clearly the legislation establishing a Martha's Vineyard Commission and the subsequent actions of the Commission brought Island Properties and the Oak Bluffs Planning Board into direct confrontation with the Commission. Island Properties, supported by the Town, maintained that its subdivision plan approved prior to the adoption of the legislation establishing the Commission permitted it to proceed with its development plan. Thus,

shortly after the Commission designated the Strock properties as a district of critical planning concern, Terrence P. McCarthy of Oak Bluffs, the sole Dukes County legislative representative, introduced a petition in the Massachusetts legislature to amend the Martha's Vineyard Commission Act. Section I of this petition stated:

"...In adopting such regulations the Commission shall not preclude building on lots lawfully laid out by plan or deed duly recorded with the Dukes County Registry of Deeds prior to July 27, 1974." [5]

Opponents of the Island Properties development plans quickly rallied support for the Commission and opposition to Representative McCarthy's proposal. On April 8, 1976, I wrote to Governor Michael Dukakis:

———————————

"I am most concerned that consideration is being given to amending the Martha's Vineyard Commission legislation in an effort to prohibit the Commission from addressing as areas of critical concern lands previously filed for subdivision. The Commission, particularly with respect to the areas around Sengekontacket, has been doing a yeoman job in endeavoring to forestall development of a very high density. Such development clearly would have a significant impact on the Island and as a practical matter make much of the Commission's other actions moot. Any amendment precluding the Commission's ability to address itself not only to

prospective developments but also those that may have been filed prior to the effective date of Chapter 637 would be most undesirable."

———————————

My letter, a copy of which also went to the Governor, to the Chairman of the Massachusetts House Committee on Natural Resources and Agriculture, stated:

———————————

"It is my understanding that your Committee is currently considering proposed amendments to Chapter 637 of the Massachusetts Laws with respect to the establishment and powers of the Martha's Vineyard Commission. I am particularly concerned that the statute not be amended in any fashion that would limit the authority of the

Commission with respect to areas where subdivision plans may have been filed and approved prior to the 1974 effective date of the statute establishing the Commission. Clearly Martha's Vineyard is too small an island to absorb the impact of that development which may have been permitted prior to 1974. In the Town of Oak Bluffs, for that matter, even before the establishment of the Commission, new zoning laws substantially altered the density requirements, but some developers filed very extensive plans just before the adoption of the new zoning limitation.

The Martha's Vineyard Commission is doing an outstanding job in evaluating areas of regional impact, and it would be highly detrimental to the efforts of the Commission if the statute were to be amended to limit its

authority with regard to plans approved prior to the effective date of the statute."

———————————————

Other overseers of the Open Land Foundation as well as residents of Harthaven similarly expressed their concern and also personally funded efforts in opposition to the extensive development proposal. The McCarthy effort to change the legislation failed. Not unexpectedly, this all ended up in litigation with the Supreme Judicial Court, the highest court in Massachusetts, ultimately (in March 1977) upholding the Commission's actions regarding the Strock properties and precluding the town of Oak Bluffs from carrying out its approval of the plans submitted by Island Properties prior to the adoption of the Commission's enabling legislation.

During the battle regarding the Strock development plans, there were efforts, spearheaded by Oak Bluffs' town leaders, to withdraw from the Commission and then to revoke the Commission's designation of the Strock Properties. These efforts, which divided the Town much as the unsuccessful 2002-2003 effort to withdraw from the Commission in connection with the proposed golf course development of the Southern Woodlands in Oak Bluffs, were rejected by the Town's voters in the Spring of 1978.

Bankruptcy of Strock Interests

As various alternatives for developing the Strock properties were being considered, the Open Land Foundation indicated an interest in purchasing the properties abutting Sengekontacket Pond with a view to limited development. In November 1974, representatives of the Foundation and the Audobon Society met with the general partners of Strock Enterprises to see whether there could be a basis for the Foundation to acquire the properties with the intention of developing up to approximately 100 house sites, completing the golf course and donating conservation easements over a substantial portion of the properties. In conjunction with those discussions, the Open Land Foundation, in consultation with Bob Fullem and me (we were each overseers of the Foundation) and Bob's friend John Williams McGrath, a professional land use planner, prepared an initial feasibility study, including estimates of costs to be incurred for matters such as roads and utilities, service for and identification of building sites, site improvements, preparation of legal documents, taxes and insurance. Unfortunately, the feasibility study prepared for the Open Land Foundation by Robert R. Kendall, a land use consultant to the Foundation, and Thomas E. Counter, the Executive Director of the Foundation, did not result in any agreement.

During the four years that the Strocks' proposal and related litigation were pending, the cost of that exercise and the attendant interest and taxes for maintaining all the Strock properties continued to rise. The result was that shortly after the Supreme Judicial Court upheld the Commission's actions regarding the Strock properties, the Bass River Savings Bank foreclosed on an over $4.5 million mortgage it held on the Strock properties, including the properties that became the Farm Neck Golf Club and its related residential properties. As was reported in the *Vineyard Gazette* of June 16, 1978,

---

"...in September, 1976 – their [the Strock interests] financial distress had become unbearable and Strock Enterprises and Island Properties asked the bankruptcy court for protection from their creditors. Both companies were declared bankrupt shortly after the court decision was handed down. As holders of a first mortgage, Bass River soon became owner of the land."

Thus a new entity now had the authority to deal with the potential development of this important area.

Aerial view (about 1976) of the recently completed new front nine holes, with the 1st hole on the lower left and a few Waterview Farm houses on the right.

Two: PURCHASE AND FOUNDING OF FARM NECK

Bass River Savings Bank promptly tried to sell the property abutting Sengekontacket Pond. While the Commission's decisions and the subsequent litigation indicated that a subdivision plan for about 250 building sites could likely be approved, the opponents of the Strock plan had indicated that there would continue to be potential opposition to any new plan of even this significant density. Thus the Bank's efforts to sell the property were hampered, as potential buyers were reluctant to invest unless they could be assured they would not be subject to the same litigation delays and costs encountered by the Strocks in their failed development efforts.

In late Spring 1977, Bob Wheeler, President of Bass River, called Bob Fullem and me to see if there could be a commitment given to a potential purchaser that there would be no opposition to a development plan for about 225 to 250 house sites. We indicated our belief that this still was greater density than seemed appropriate for the Sengekontacket area properties and that something more in the range of 100 house sites would be significantly less likely to draw opposition. Mr. Wheeler said that he did not think that was a feasible development density to attract a buyer willing to pay what the Bank expected to realize for the property. After several months, Mr. Wheeler called to ask whether Bob and I would be interested in purchasing the property. We both said, "We're New York lawyers, not developers. We enjoy going to the Vineyard for vacation in the summers. Moreover we hardly have either the time or expertise necessary to even consider buying the properties." Mr. Wheeler persevered, however, and suggested that at least we meet with him at the Bank to see if there were any ways in which the Bank might proceed in selling the properties.

Negotiating an Option

After extended discussions, in early summer of 1977 Bob and I outlined a proposal to the Bank: If the Bank would give us a six months' option to buy the properties at a price that could be agreed upon, we would try to develop a plan for the purchase of the properties by a group of individuals who would have an interest in preserving as much open space as possible on the properties. We said we would not pay anything for the option and we would try to formulate a purchase plan that would not require any financing other than the commitment of individuals who might participate in the purchase. It was understood that the Bank could continue to try to market the properties pending a definitive agreement.

Since the objective of negotiating an option was to assure limited development, we contemplated trying to enlist the support of about 40 individuals interested in conservation. Our concept was that sufficient commitments would be needed to pay the purchase price to Bass River and to have sufficient additional funds to build the second nine holes for the contemplated new 18-hole golf course (Island Properties had built a new nine before going bankrupt), to develop and obtain approvals of a house sites plan and to build roads and utilities infrastructure.

As our proposal was fleshed out, we decided that no more than 49 house sites would be contemplated and that scenic easements and development rights would be donated to provide charitable contributions for much of the properties not needed for house sites. Our plan also assumed we could find buyers for the motel and restaurant at the old Island Country Club and the two Strock farm houses on the property. We then set about trying to enlist potential participants. In concept, each participant would be asked to invest $50,000 for the opportunity to own a building site, to become a stockholder in the yet to be completed golf course and to share in the potential income tax benefits of the proposed charitable donation. The overarching objective was to have as limited development as would permit the purchase and related efforts and to break even in the process. It may well be the only development project without a profit motive.

We prepared a very preliminary outline of our idea in July 1977 and circulated copies to individuals we thought might have an interest in supporting the concept:

OUTLINE OF PROPOSED PURCHASE OF SENGEKONTACKET PROPERTIES

Approximately 550 acres of land in Oak Bluffs and Edgartown abutting Sengekontacket Pond, formerly owned by the Strock interests, are expected to be offered for sale by the Bass River Savings Bank after it acquires the properties in August or September in foreclosure of its mortgage on the properties. The land lying in Oak Bluffs is covered by an approved sub-division plan involving approximately 875 single-family lots. The Martha's Vineyard Commission has directed that the lot density be no greater than one and one-half acres per each lot, approximately 350 lots for all the land involved.

Aerial view (about 1976) of the 4th hole, with the 5th fairway on the right and Waterview Farm houses at the top left.

It is proposed that a group of up to 50 persons purchase the entire property from Bass River. The purchase price is expected to be between $1,500,000 and $2,000,000. The land would be master planned into approximately 50 single-family building sites. The average size of the lots would be between 2 and 3 acres. Consideration will also be given to some low-cost Island Resident parcels. The second nine holes of the golf course would be completed immediately if sufficient funds are available or later on as an alternative plan. Approximately 150-200 acres would be devoted to the golf course and recreational facilities. The remaining 200-250 acres would be donated to a non-profit institution or institutions. This donation of land is expected to be valued at $500,000 - $1,000,000.

The cost of improving each building site with roads, water and electricity is estimated to be no more than $5,000 per site. The golf course construction is expected to cost approximately $250,000. The total cost of master planning, site improvements and other costs involved should not exceed $500,000, or $750,000 with the completion of the golf course. Accordingly, the average cost of each site to the purchasers would be $45,000 to $50,000.

After the site planning has been completed, a minimum price for each site in the range of $30,000-$65,000 will be established. The aggregate minimum cost of all sites will cover the total cost of the project ($2,250,000 - $2,500,000). The purchasers will be permitted to bid for the sites. The bid process will result in each purchaser acquiring title to one site. The golf course and recreational land will be conveyed to a separate corporation which will be owned mutually by the site owners.

Bass River will be requested to agree to lend approximately 60-70% of the purchase price to each individual purchaser if desired by the purchaser. Accordingly, the expected economics for each purchaser will be as follows:

Purchase Price . . . . $1,500,000 – $2,000,000
Site Cost . . . . 750,000 – 500,000
Subscription . . . . 45,000 – 50,000
Cash Required: All Cash: . . . . 45,000 – 50,000
                     With Financing: . . . . 13,500 – 15,000
Mortgage Note: . . . . 31,500 – 35,000
Donation Tax Deduction: . . . . 10,000 – 20,000

Net Cash Investment After Donation
(assuming donation deduction at 50% tax rate):
 . . . . .8,500 – 10,000 (tax credit $5,000)
With financing: . . . . 3,500 – 5,000 (tax credit $10,000)

In front page article of July 22, 1977 in the *Vintage Gazette* entitled "'Rescue Plan' for Waterview Acreage is Mounted by Group of Island Investors", written by Henry Beetle Hough, it was reported:

"What is in effect a rescue operation for some 550 acres abutting Sengekontacket Pond now in foreclosure proceedings brought by the Bass River Bank is proposed by a group being formally organized on the Vineyard. The

proposal is designed to substitute for the old intensive development planned by the Strock interests, an entirely new plan with minimal development consistent with sound management, completion of the golf course, and the setting aside of extensive acreage for conservation.

Informal conversations have been held with the Bass River Savings Bank, and the new group hopes that a formal proposal may be submitted to the Bank in August."

With hindsight, particularly recognizing the exponential escalation in Martha's Vineyard property values over the last decade, the prospect of enlisting support for this project would seem to have been a slam-dunk. In the economic reality of 1977 and 1978, however, the prospect of inducing individuals to pay an average $50,000 each proved daunting indeed. The challenge was singularly difficult because there was only a concept – basically we asked for a commitment with a "trust us and we'll build a fine course, identify house sites, do the necessary work on roads and utilities and we'll assure you will get a good tax deduction." While we were not surprised that there was not a rush to join us in our dream, our dedication to trying to save this beautiful property kept us motivated and optimistic.

Enlisting Participants

The July 22, 1977 article in the *Vineyard Gazette* about this project caught the attention of Douglass Mabee, a gentleman in Edgartown who had recently retired. Doug had been a salesman for 25 years for National Folding Box, a family company that merged with Federal Paper Board Company, and had also been a founder of Stratton Mountain ski area in Vermont. Out of the blue, Doug called me to say that he would like to help if help were needed in what he understood sounded like a very interesting project. Volunteers were short indeed and Doug was welcomed with open arms. After his first look at the new nine holes of the golf course that had been completed in 1976, Doug was struck by the beauty of the property, noting, "...the ponds, marshland, the gently undulating land, pine forests, ever-present geese, this just had to be preserved from the quarter acre development that had earlier received approval by the town fathers in Oak Bluffs." He soon became so enthusiastic that for the next several months he spent almost full time showing the Farm Neck property to a number of his friends in Edgartown and acquaintances from many other areas as well. His enthusiasm knew no bounds. While so many of the people he took to Farm Neck were impressed by the beauty of the property and fully supported the limited development concept intended to preserve as much open space as possible, he was consistently disappointed, but undaunted, by the failure of so many to be willing to commit to become participants in the purchase. Doug's percentage of success enlisting participation by the many he took to see the property was small indeed, yet he nevertheless was responsible for enlisting a number of the participants who ultimately made the Farm Neck purchase possible. Most of the people who were encouraged by Doug were solely interested in the conservation aspects of the proposal and included leading Island conservationists such as Mary Wakeman, Maitland Edey and Farleigh Dickinson.

As Doug scoured the Island for potential support of the effort to acquire the Strock properties, he contacted each of the local conservation groups. As he recalled in a memoir he wrote after completion of the Farm Neck purchase:

———————————

"In the initial phase of our contact with the local conservation groups it didn't take us long to realize that each, in its wondrous ways, had their own individual approach to a common goal. While we unquestionably had their support and encouragement, support did not mean participation. Participation remained an individual decision."

———————————

The one exception eventually was the Vineyard Open Land Foundation (VOLF), which had studied the Waterview properties several years earlier. Under the leadership of its president, Bob Lawrence, VOLF and Rob Kendall worked with Bob, Doug and me to update its 1974-1975 feasibility study and to prepare the outline of a plan to help enlist support for purchase of the Strock properties. One of the questions that had to be addressed was how to pay VOLF for the cost of preparing the study. A practical solution occurred to Bob and me, so we promptly wrote to each of the potential participants to encourage them to make a tax deductible contribution of "at least $100 (and preferably $200)" to the Foundation. My letter of September 23, 1977 to potential participants said:

———————————

"The objectives of the Open Land Foundation are of course very comparable to those of our own group. As most of you know, the Foundation makes every effort to assist in planning, consulting and, in limited cases, implementation of the land programs directed to

preserving environmentally and ecologically important areas while at the same time recognizing the need for limited development in some instances. Although its programs are on a broader scale than our group's proposed Sengekontacket properties purchase, we hope that each of the proposed participants in our proposed purchase program would make a donation of at least $100 (and preferably $200 if possible), in recognition of the important role that the Foundation is playing on the Vineyard. Such a contribution would, of course, be a deductible charitable contribution,...

————————————————————

Happily, sufficient funds were donated to cover the costs of the feasibility study.

The Vineyard Conservation Society in its Fall 1977 Newsletter supported the project with kind words but without active further involvement. The Newsletter ends with "...if a realistic basis for purchase can be negotiated this plan [Farm Neck] will succeed, to the great profit of the Island and as a landmark step in imaginative and sensitive land use. The VCS applauds the effort and this plan."

Among the many people Doug Mabee approached to enlist their support of the purchase of the Strock properties, Doug noted in his memoir:

————————————————————

"No man stands as tall, in my estimation, as Henry Beetle Hough, the 'Country Editor'. No single person gave as much encouragement. I became a frequent visitor to the Gazette,

just a short hop on the bicycle from our house on South Water Street. I would feed Henry and Dick Reston (the editor) maps, progress reports and photographs. They or George Adams and others would fashion the articles and Henry the editorials."

In Henry Beetle Hough's September 27, 1977 article in the *Vineyard Gazette* entitled "Strock Property Bid Awaits Sale" he added his prestige and support of our budding efforts:

"The auction of former Strock and Island Properties land advertised by the Bass River Savings Bank to take place on Sept. 29 as a results of foreclosure proceedings may bring closer the accomplishment of the "rescue" plan organized under the leadership of Douglass W. Mabee, Charles H. Harff

and others. If, as widely believed, it is now unrealistic to expect bidding on the scale of the total mortgage indebtedness, the next step would be one of negotiation by the bank.

Meantime, the participating group in the rescue plan is 80 percent completed. A time lapse of six months following the auction date is anticipated before a definite decision is likely to be made by the bank.

A summary of the rescue plan as it now stands shows that Felix Neck may receive a substantial gift of property abutting Major's Cove, contiguous with the present Felix Neck preserve. This is part of the 550-acre tract on the slope of Sengekontacket Pond which extends from the Island Country Club through the former Luce and Love farms.

Aerial view (about 1976) of the 9th hole and the intended one-acre double green, with the proposed 18th green on the left. The green eventually was split and a pond created in front of the two greens.

This is an area of great beauty and of environmental importance. Extensive salt marshes all along the pond provide nutrients for varied fowl, fish and shellfish. It is urged that proper use of the property is essential if the pond's important ecological functions are not to be marred by contamination.

This is the region on which a high density development of 867 lots of about a quarter-acre each on 507 acres had been proposed and initially approved by the Oak Bluffs planning board because of a legal limitation on its powers. Only the timely intervention of the Martha's Vineyard Commission prevented execution of the development plan.

The aim of the civic and environmentally concerned group now 80 percent formed is to find a responsible solution for the Sengekontacket properties. The group's basic concept, if it can

negotiate a realistic purchase from the bank, is to limit the number of house sites to 60 or 70, retain the new nine-hole golf course completed in 1976, complete the initially planned other nine holes, and, most importantly, to donate between 200 and 250 acres to Felix Neck and other conservation entities.

If this conservation plan succeeds, only about 150 to 200 acres would actually be used for home sites and roads, so that a significant part of the area would retain its ecological and scenic values to the Island. Another benefit would be augmenting the nature and bridle trails of the region.

This overall plan is intended to offer a practical alternative to high density commercial development of the properties, the proponents say. Although representatives of the group have held discussions with the Bass River bank, up to now *there has been no agreement on price that would enable a proposed essentially non-profit plan to succeed. Discussions are continuing, and the Vineyard Conservation Society is hopeful that what it regards as an imaginative plan can be accomplished."*

In our letter of March 24, 1978 to proposed participants, we advised:

"Since our last communication to you, we have received a Feasibility Study prepared by the Vineyard Open Land Foundation covering the various parcels of former Strock Properties abutting Sengekontacket Pond that our group has proposed to endeavor to purchase from Bass River Savings Bank. The study, which has been very well done indeed and goes into considerable detail on estimated costs for roads, water, electrical and telephone, site improvements, surveying, taxes, insurance, legal work, construction engineering and other matters, basically confirms the estimates that we had made last summer on a much less detailed basis. We are, thus, confident that if the property can be purchased from the Bank at a price in the range of $1,500,000 to $1,800,000, the program proposed last summer can be carried out on a realistic and successful basis.

Although of course no one can give any absolute assurance in this regard, we are gratified that the report also tends to confirm that the estimated site values after the development of the properties along the lines we have suggested would support a purchase price in the range we are considering.

We now understand that Bass River intends to make up its mind as to the sale of this property in May. Although we are skeptical as to whether the Bank in fact will do so, and even more skeptical as to whether the Bank has other offers as its President has indicated, we nevertheless believe that a formal letter should be submitted confirming our group's interest."

———————————————————

One of the difficult issues in forming a purchaser group was how to allocate the various home sites, particularly without an approved site development plan. Initially it was contemplated that home sites would be selected by a lottery; then there was consideration of an auction among the participants; and finally, by specific site selections by the participants. The latter recognized that while each of the sites had a view of Sengekontacket Pond, the aesthetics were different,

depending for example on whether a participant was more interested in a golf course view or a view of open meadows or marshland. In recognition of the variances in the proposed house lots, different values, ranging from $40,000 to $56,000, but nevertheless maintaining an average of $50,000 were determined. Potential participants thus were able to select particular locations on the conceptual building lots outlined in the VOLF study. While this seemed a reasonable and relatively simple approach, it turned out to have a number of problems as new prospects decided that they really would only participate if they could have a particular lot already selected by an earlier participant. Luckily, a number of early participants, whose primary interest was conservation, were willing to give up lots they had selected and to take another lot so that additional participants could be secured. Certainly Maitland Edey was a most gracious example as he willingly gave up one lot after another to accommodate new prospects. As Doug Mabee recalled, "I asked Mait Edey so many times I was embarrassed to ask him, yet again." Clearly Mait Edey's interest in Farm Neck was solely conservation and he, among several others, including Bob Fullem and I made Farm Neck a reality by subscribing to two lots.

Among Doug's memoir recollections in describing the mid-Summer 1978 difficulties of attracting enough support, he noted:

———————————————————

"It was now mid-July and still no progress in obtaining additional participants beyond that plateau of 30/35. It seemed an impassable barrier — the only thing that showed an increase was our list of refusals! Perhaps a cocktail party might help….and what better place to hold one than the Alvin Strock

farmhouse! Everyone would be exposed to the environment we hoped to preserve and we'd have a captive audience no distractions. Prue and I went to work. The farmhouse was a mess — so overgrown one couldn't enter the front door. Lisha Smith, whose family is deeply rooted in Farm Neck history and with whom Tim Mabee had worked at Mattakesett, came with his 'brush hog' $45 = Truck loads of brush were removed and finally the house could be seen for the authentic 'Cape' it was. Invitations were mailed to 150 — one-third that number attended — but disappointingly, no converts."

———————————————————

Another individual whose enthusiasm, as well as experience, had a great deal to do with the success in finding participants for the Farm Neck purchase was John Williams McGrath. John had worked on several golf course development projects for the

Rockefellers including Mauna Kea in Hawaii and Fountain Valley on St. Croix; and he had become a good friend of Bob Fullem whose firm handled the legal work for those projects. John had also been very much involved in the development of Hilton Head. In any event when John first heard about Bob's and my proposal to acquire the Farm Neck properties, and after he saw the properties, he readily enlisted others to become participants. Equally important, John had substantial experience in golf course development and recommended Patrick Mulligan, a friend with whom he had worked, to serve as the architect for the new nine holes that would be built to complete the 18-hole course if, as and when the purchase were completed.

Shortly after the cocktail party failed to produce additional participants, Bob arranged for John to visit the property, with Doug as tour guide. As Doug noted in his recollections,

---

"I can remember, as yesterday, watching John scramble up a huge boulder for a better view of Farm Neck. He couldn't believe what he saw. Here, nature had provided all the elements which the golf course architect tries to accomplish artificially in Florida, with berms, earth moving equipment, pot holes, bulkheads, lagoons, etc... and the price... unbelievable! His enthusiasm and reaction was the same as had prompted me..."

When John returned to his office in New York he extolled Farm Neck in such glowing terms that Gerald Hines, a major developer of office and retail complexes in cities such as Atlanta and Houston, asked John what this project was all about. This was followed up by Doug being alerted to the

Aerial view (about 1976) of the 7th hole and the 8th tees (foreground).

fact that he could expect a call from Mr. Hines. Doug recalled the meeting in his memoir as follows:

———————————

"8:00 a.m. 'This is Gerald Hines in Houston. Can you meet us at the Vineyard airport at 1:30? I'll be picking up a friend in Chicago. What's the weather like up there? We can only stay a short while, as we have to be back in New York for a 4:30 appointment.'

'Dull and overcast with rain expected.' – Great!

Prue made sandwiches, soup and I put some Bloody Marys in a couple of thermoses and off we went to the airport. How would we recognize Hines and friend? Why naturally he'd be a tall Texan in a suede jacket wearing cowboy boots.

'I'm just a country boy, green as I can be.'

The Lear jet touched down at precisely 1:30 and out stepped a fellow in a business suit, more slightly built than I, wearing Gucci's! What the hell is this? I was wearing my usual 'Easterner' red pants, guaranteed to fade, L.L. Bean boots and yellow slicker. One of the airport attendants exclaimed 'only two passengers on that plane.'

We toured the perimeters in Prue's 230 Diesel. It was pouring by then, the car windows were steamed, and at best one could only sense the terrain and physical features of Farm Neck. We had provided extra Bean boots, umbrellas, rain gear, but they were of no use in the deluge. A 'goodlie' fire was burning in the kitchen of the old 'Cape' by the 7th – that Rumford fireplace could handle whole logs, trunks or even foots of trees – no split wood needed. After lunch it was time to return to the airport. The '4:30 appointment' was in actuality a cocktail party! How's that for a day's schedule! On the way I asked if they'd mind signing the contract – no problem. The friend was a former associate of Hines' from the Chicago days, Robert Barton, then head of Rock Resorts, Woodstock, VT."

In a short time John McGrath's contacts produced seven additional participants, including several business associates of Gerald Hines. One of them called Bob Fullem to ask about signing the necessary papers. When Bob asked, "Have you seen the property?", he said, "No, but where do I sign?" Bob asked, "Have you received and read the brochure describing the proposed project?" He said, "No, but where do I sign? If Gerry Hines is in, so am I." With the addition of this new group of investors, together with others attracted by Bob and me, the group was then large enough to go forward with the purchase.

Signing the Purchase Contract

In a letter of April 24, 1978, Messrs. Fullem, Harff and Mabee wrote to the President of Bass River Savings Bank stating:

"Although we have for almost a year discussed with you the serious interest that we and a group of associates have in purchasing from Bass River Savings Bank the properties acquired on foreclosure of its mortgage of certain so-called Strock Properties bordering Sengekontacket Pond, we wish to confirm formally the offer made during the summer of 1977 so that you and

your Board of Directors can act thereon."

――――――――――――――

After setting forth the terms of the proposed offer for approximately 550 acres of the Strock properties, the letter concluded:

――――――――――――――

"We wish again to note for you and your Board's consideration the fact that our group's primary interest in purchasing this property is to preserve the natural beauty and character of the Vineyard generally, and certainly particularly the area abutting Sengekontacket Pond. The limited development we propose, as well as the significant charitable donation contemplated, clearly demonstrate that objective. We have had a detailed study made of the property and believe that the price being

offered represents full value, bearing in mind particularly environmental and sociological factors limiting development of this property. We hope that the Bank would give our offer serious consideration and will be willing to meet with you or the Board should you wish to discuss our proposal."

――――――――――――――

The *Vineyard Gazette*, on June 16, 1978, reported in a front-page article entitled "Limited Sengekontacket Plan is Aim of New Agreement" that:

――――――――――――――

"The Bass River Savings Bank and Island conservation interests have reached agreement-in-principle on a plan that would preserve a large portion of the Waterview Farms on the western shore of Sengekontacket Pond.

The plan provides for limited development of the 550-acre tract to finance preservation of the remainder. The new Island Country Club golf course would be completed. The restaurant and motel on the tract would remain in operation.

The proposed transaction includes the Waterview III, IV, and VI developments which Bass River became owner of after the bankruptcies of Strock Enterprises and Island Properties.

It includes all of Bass River's holdings in the area except for a few scattered lots in Waterview II.

❖ ❖ ❖

Charles Harff and Robert Fullem, both of New York and Oak Bluffs, lead the loosely-constructed group which has offered to purchase the Bass River Property. Their interest in preserving the land began in 1974 when, as overseers of the Vineyard Open Land Foundation (VOLF) they attempted to forestall the major development of the area the Strock interests has in mind.

❖ ❖ ❖

Douglas A. Mabee, a participant in the Farm Neck group, said Tuesday that the group's plan has not changed significantly since it was first proposed to the bank a year ago.

The group is seeking a total of 46 participants, each of whom will purchase rights to one house site on the property. The funds will be used to purchase the land outright from the bank; to complete development of the property; and to complete the golf course.

◆ ◆ ◆

As holder of a first mortgage, Bass River soon became owner of the land. 'We had a dozen or more parties interested in the land, but in their opinion none of them could go through the necessary process of commission approval,' Mr. Wheeler said this Wednesday. 'The plan Mr. Harff and Mr. Fullem propose will not require any further approval by the commission. Their plan is consistent with the desires of a lot of people on the Island and of the commission,' Mr. Wheeler said.

Given the mission of the commission – which I am not at odds with – there were very few solutions to the problem. This solution has to be a plus for the Island and we are very pleased to have a resolution for the property,' he said."

―――――――――――――――――

Henry Beetle Hough continued his support of the effort to save these properties from over-development with his editorial of June 20, 1978:

―――――――――――――――――

"The New Farm Neck
The plan for limited development of some 500 acres on the slopes of Sengekontacket Pond, replacing the intensive 867-lot development struck down by the Martha's Vineyard Commission and a supporting decision of the Supreme Judicial Court of the state, is remarkable for a number of reasons. First of all it is remarkable because the function of the entrepreneur is replaced by dedication to the interest of the Island. Broadly speaking, there is no "developer"; instead, there is a joint enterprise for enlightened planning of an Island tract and an Island landscape.

In this planning the Vineyard Open Land Foundation has had a part. The Vineyard Conservation Society has entered into the discussions and may be instrumental in adapting the same concept to another endangered region.

Short of outright purchase of open spaces on a scale not only impossible but socially and economically undesirable, this proposed method seems the one recourse to assure wise use of land and a proper relationship between "development" and open space. The phrase "seems to be" is used because the plan is not yet certain of accomplishment.

It requires the participation of investors and a large infusion of public spirit. This, then, is the most urgent test of a concept long discussed and now put forward in practical terms for the first time.

The christening of the enterprise with the name Farm Neck is historically sound and properly symbolic of its Vineyard sinews. According to the account of Dr. Banks, the region was called Farm Neck for the first time in the records of 1703, and "this name has clung to it with a tenacity which time and a newer and fancier name cannot sever." The name was derived "from the first grant of 500 acres made in 1642 to John Daggett 'for a farm,' which covered the present settlement of Oak Bluffs.

According to Henry Franklin Norton's history, 'When Joseph Norton built at Farm Neck he could count more than 40 wigwams looking from his back door toward Sengekontacket Pond' However this may have seemed at the time, it may now be taken as a prototype of limited development."

After further discussion and negotiation, an agreement in principle was executed on June 27, 1978 in which the Bank agreed to sell to the proposed purchaser group "between 540 and 570 acres" for $1.825 million plus one single-family home site on the property to be developed. The agreement in principle provided a definitive agreement setting forth the complete terms and conditions of the purchase must be executed by July 31, 1978 and retained the right of the Bank "to continue to market the properties" and to sell the properties to others at any time prior to closing "on such terms as Bass River in its sole discretion deems at least as favorable to it as those set forth herein."

At the end of July 1978, Henry Beetle Hough once again lent his considerable prestige and support to the Farm Neck rescue effort in the following *Vineyard Gazette* editorial:

"Urgent

That area, critical to the integrity and quality of the Vineyard, 500 acres of beautiful land on the slopes of Sengekontacket Pond, on which an intensive development of 867 lots was planned, has not yet been rescued. It still stands in peril and the month of August may be decisive as to its future.

Last June, with summer just coming on, announcement was made of an agreement in principle between the Bass River Savings Bank and an Island group joining in an innovative plan for purchase by its members, a dramatically reduced intensity of land use, assured continuance of the new Martha's Vineyard Country Club golf course, and dedication of large and vitally important areas to open space preservation. This last element of the plan of course made possible an attractive advantage to members of the group, along with the obvious motive of public spirit.

With the end of July close at hand, how has this New Farm Neck project been getting on? It has made what must have been considered only a few months ago amazing progress. It seems to stand within reach of a goal of great Island concern. But the goal has not been reached. More members must be added to the purchasing group.

The necessary support cannot be obtained by a whoop-it-up campaign or any widespread solicitation. Investors are sought whose purposes will join appropriately in the overall design, a matter that must be decided individually. The success of the concept itself seems to run without limit in significance.

Should it fail, the Island would have lost its only alternative preservation. Should it succeed, a precedent would have been established in which lovers of the Island could take heart, raising the prospect of rescue for more endangered acreage.

Summer is the season of looking at land, the season of yearning and of the liveliest impulses of acquisition. If enough of these match the advantages of the New Farm Neck purchase, then August can see the success of a project following in direct line from the work of the Open Land Foundation and the Vineyard Conservation Society."

On August 3, 1978, a definitive purchase and sale agreement for the Strock properties was executed between Bass River Savings Bank and Messrs. Fullem, Harff and Mabee, the general partners of Farm Neck Associates (a limited partnership organized to effect the purchase). A closing was to be held no later than September 29, 1978. The agreement was conditioned, among other things, on the buyers obtaining commitments from participants to purchase not less than 44 of the 49 lots to be created at Farm Neck.

Henry Beetle Hough continued his support of the Farm Neck project with a low key editorial in August 1978:

———————————

"How Many Have Been There?

A timely question is just this: Have you been to Farm Neck? Everyone has seen Farm Neck, dozens of times, oftener than can be computed. From the Beach Road between Edgartown and Oak Bluffs one looks across Sengekontacket Pond at the rising land on the other side. Northward of Major's Cove and extending to and beyond the limit of the pond lies Farm Neck, an epitome of scenery and history that has had too little attention. The name does not even appear in the index of the Banks history of the Vineyard. Henry Franklin Norton treats it in picturesque instances in his history, but does not say just where it is.

Everyone has looked at Farm Neck across the pond, but how many have been there? Knowing Farm Neck is of critical importance now because the future of its openness, its ponds, declivities, trees, and marshes, the whole quality and livability of the region, will soon be decided.

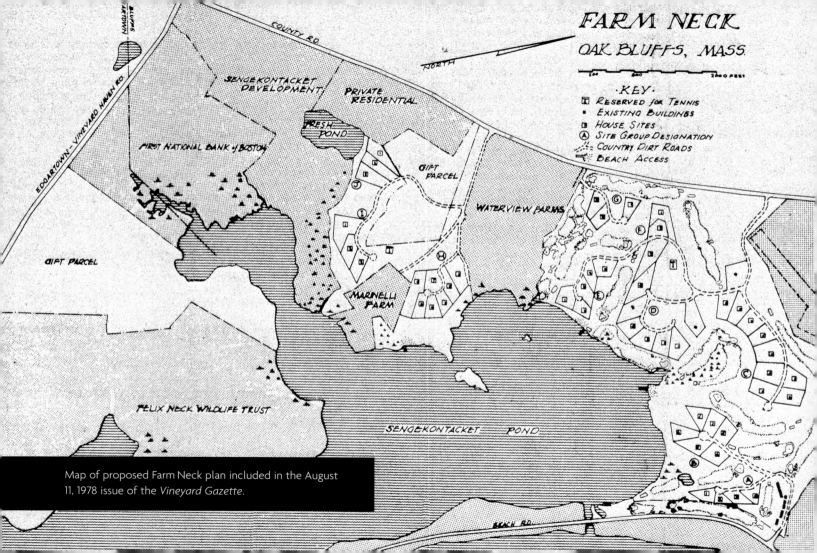

Map of proposed Farm Neck plan included in the August 11, 1978 issue of the *Vineyard Gazette*.

The new Farm Neck Association has a plan for limited development and broadly conceived preservation of the land on the northwestern shore of Sengekontacket Pond. The Association has entered into a purchase and sale agreement with the Bass River Savings Bank covering the former Waterview III, IV and VI developments on which the bank holds a mortgage. Fewer than 50 lots are planned in a region that had been divided into almost a thousand. The new lots are mostly of two to three acres, with a few larger ones, and Waterview VI is conceived as undeveloped and dedicated to preservation.

Some may be interested to participate in the plan and some may not. There's no pressure as to that. But Farm Neck is worth seeing, and the time is now.

So the question hangs in the air of August, 1978: Have you been to Farm Neck?"

———————————————————

The August 11, 1978 issue of the *Vineyard Gazette* contained an article entitled "Farm Neck Unveils Plan" and included a map of the proposed development that showed proposed building sites, roads and gift parcels. The article reported that:

———————————————————

"The Farm Neck Association unveiled its tentative plot plan for limited development of the northwestern shore of Sengekontacket Pond this weekend, at the first meeting of its participants.

The Association has entered a purchase and sale agreement with the Bass River Savings Bank for the Waterview III, IV and VI developments planned by the now-bankrupt Strock family interests. The Association plans to finance the purchase by limited development – less than 50 lots – of an area which had been divided into nearly 1,000 lots.

Charles Harff, one of the leaders of the effort, said this weekend that the method of distributing lots among participants has been changed. Originally it was planned that each participant would pay $50,000 for rights to an unspecified lot, and the lots would be allocated after the purchase.

Recognizing that there is some value difference among the lots, Mr. Harff said, the lots have now been differentially priced, and participants will choose a lot at the time they become participants. Four of the lots are now priced at $40,000; four at $45,000; ten are priced at $56,000; and the remainder are priced at $50,000. Mr. Harff points out that 80 per cent of the lots remain priced at $50,000 or less.

Mr. Harff said that the list of participants continues to grow, and that he is hopeful of completing the purchase by the deadline at the end of September.

The success at enlisting participants encourages him, he said, about the basic soundness of the idea: 'Trying to save land and break even doing it'."

Completing the Purchase

We continued with great optimism to endeavor to complete the group necessary for our purchase. As a "fail safe" we also explored possible bridge financing should it be needed, which at the end it was not. the *Vineyard Gazette* continued to monitor and encourage our progress. In its September 5, 1978 edition, it reported:

"Farm Neck Hopes High

Leaders of the Farm Neck group expressed optimism this weekend about the prospects of their plan for limited development of the erstwhile Waterview Farms properties on the north side of Sengekontacket Pond.

Charles H. Harff said Saturday, "We are confident we are going to be able to close the transaction with the bank, but we still need a few more participants."

The group has obtained a purchase option from the Bass River Savings Bank which acquired the property through a mortgage foreclosure when Strock Enterprises and Island Properties went bankrupt last year. The option expires Sept. 29.

The Strock plans for the property involved a subdivision of nearly 1,000 lots. The Farm Neck group plans a clustered subdivision of about 50 lots of roughly two acres each. The golf course will be completed, and the remainder of the land will be devoted to conservation.

The purchase and limited development are being financed by participants who, for a fee ranging from $40,000 to $56,000, acquire an interest in the project and rights to one of the lots.

Mr. Harff points out that the total cost of the plan is much lower than the cost a commercial developer would incur on the same property. The capital cost is less, and the interest costs are borne by the individual participant when he mortgages his lot. Costs of utilities and roads are substantially smaller because there are fewer lots to service. Finally, marketing costs — which in a commercial development are a major portion of the total cost — are negligible in this plan.

As a means of saving land for conservation purposes, Mr. Harff also says this method has the advantage that it does not depend on donations. When the undeveloped land is given to a non-profit institution for protection, each participant acquires a tax deduction. The participant winds up with a lot of value equal to or greater than his cost of participation."

Unfortunately, when the closing date arrived, the title insurance company had not been able to resolve an issue with respect to a portion of the land to be transferred, so all the parties agreed to defer the closing for three weeks while that issue was resolved. Moreover, at about the last minute before the scheduled September 29 closing date, two prospective participants whom Doug Mabee had introduced changed their minds and revoked their commitments. Even though there were no new prospects readily available, we refunded to each of the persons who withdrew the $2,500 they had paid when signing their participation contracts. Considering the ultimate value of the Farm Neck house sites[8], hopefully each of them eventually learned how great a mistake they made in withdrawing. In any event, the scramble to find two new prospects continued up to and for a short time after the closing.

On October 20, 1978 the purchase was completed. Farm Neck Associates paid the Bank $1.5 million and assigned to the Bank its contract for the sale for $325,000 of the motel/restaurant and its site on about 6.8 acres. Once again, Henry Beetle Hough penned a very supportive editorial, praising the effort in the October 27, 1978 edition of the *Vineyard Gazette*:

"New on a Fair Horizon

The New Farm Neck project victory is a gain for all of Martha's Vineyard and a flare of hope in the sky for the future. This will become more and more apparent as the whole significance of the victory settles in and, what may take even longer, the details of the concept are carried into fuller realization.

The Farm Neck Association, as it was first called, has concluded the agreement envisioned last summer when a tentative arrangement was reached with the Bass River Savings Bank for limited development of the Waterview III, IV and VI projects of the Strock family. Under this plan there will be something like 50 lots instead of almost a thousand, with a major acreage preserved for conservation. If the early plans are carried out, lots will be of two or three acres with some of larger size, all related to the particular environment. The Waterview VI region has been envisioned as entirely free of development.

If any similar concept of such size and provision for the public interest has ever been brought to success on the Island, none can now be remembered, and none that even approaches this in any of its aspects and dimensions.

Many months of dedicated effort have been devoted to the plan, the winning of necessary support, and the complexities necessary for its execution. Recognition of those who have sustained the plan and carried it forward should be given and will be given. The names of Mabee, Harff, Fullem, and Edey occur inevitably, not necessarily in this order. A round robin form of credit would probably be more fair, and other names should be included.

Meantime Vineyarders may well visit the New Farm Neck or view it from any point of vantage, seeing the region under

the golden October sunlight in a fairness of prospect coming down from early times, secure for the future through vision and effort that from now on will seem more promising and more worthy of support than in the sadder viewpoint of the past."

The final actions to complete the Farm Neck purchase were distribution of the building lots to the participants once necessary planning board approvals were obtained, organization of the golf course corporation and distribution of stock in that corporation to participants, donation of portions of the acquired properties and related development rights, and obtaining planned tax deductions for the participants. All this was completed by 1982, the last item being a letter of April 2, 1982 in which the IRS advised Farm Neck Associates that its tax return for the year ended December 31, 1979, had been accepted as filed. Since this was the year in which Farm Neck made its outright donation to Felix Neck (described later) and placed conservation easements on significant additional properties, this was an important last step in the completion of the Farm Neck project. It should be noted that R. M. Bradley & Co., Inc. a leading real estate appraisal firm in Boston MA, appraised the value of the properties donated at $2.402 million, thus giving each participant in the Farm Neck purchase a tax deduction nearly equal to the individual's investment.

In our letter of March 19, 1980 to Farm Neck's Limited Partners we commented (rather conservatively when viewed with hindsight):

"The R. M. Bradley appraisal report is in part predicated on values of recent relatively comparable lot sales. Thus, R. M. Bradley has assumed that lots in the Farm Neck project can be expected to have resale values in the range of $70,000 to $80,000. While we cannot, of course, give any guidance as to prices at which any of you may wish to sell your lot, it should be noted that any sales substantially below the projected values could have an adverse effect on resolution of questions that the Internal Revenue Service might raise regarding the value of the gifts to Felix Neck. While we understand several sales to be under consideration, the only completed one of which we know took place late in December when lot D-3 was sold for $82,500. Obviously, further sales within or above the price ranges estimated by the Bradley firm can only serve to buttress the conclusions of the appraisers."

Aerial view (about 1976) of the 3rd hole on the right and 5th hole on the left.

Of course by the time the IRS proposed to audit and contest the appraisal, values had already risen. When we advised the IRS that we'd file an amended appraisal claiming a donation value in excess of $4 million, the IRS quickly withdrew its challenge of the original appraisal. We were grateful for the tax planning expertise and guidance provided by Fenton Burke, one of Bob's partners at Dewey, Ballantine and one of the initial participants in the Farm Neck purchase.

In an article of January 11, 1980 encapsulating the success of the Farm Neck effort, the *Vineyard Gazette* included the following:

"For Charles H. Harff and L. Robert Fullem, corporate lawyers from New York City and Waterview home owners, the completion of the plans on schedule and within a budget of several million dollars, marks the good end to a land use struggle. Mr. Harff and Mr. Fullem are general partners in Farm Neck Associates as is Douglas W. Mabee of Edgartown.

◆ ◆ ◆

The property was purchased for $1.5 million; the three general partners figured another million would be needed to complete the plans.

'We were trying to sell participation in a project by saying, "If you give us $50,000, we think you'll get your money back,"' Mr. Harff said yesterday from his Manhattan law office. 'We just wanted the land developed in as limited a fashion as possible to break even. We went into this to save a very significant piece of property which we thought had substantial interest on the Island. I think we've fully met our objectives in all directions.'

Two non-golfers enjoying Farm Neck, part of what so much attracted Doug Mabee to help.

There was never any motive for profit, neither was there any experience in land use design or development. For that, the partners relied upon Robert Kendall for the plotting of the property and Timothy Sweet, the association's general manager, for the completion of all details, large and small.

'I've never seen anything done with this big a piece of land when the bottom profit line wasn't the focus,' Mr. Sweet said. 'I can see how a great deal of money could have been made by a developer.'"

Henry Beetle Hough followed up this laudatory article in an editorial in the January 18, 1980 edition of the *Vineyard Gazette* entitled "Imaginative Concept Realized":

"There's so much in the Farm Neck land project – land and water project, really – that it is hard to take in at one sitting. Most Vineyarders sooner or later will want to go out and see for themselves what has, in the old phrase, been brought to pass. One might say marvelously brought to pass. Douglass Mabee says it all began with a remark made to him by Phil Combra in Bert's Barber Shop three years ago. Phil spoke of the recreational possibilities of the Strock land in the Sengekontacket region which had been marked out for intensive housing development, a sub-division into 840 half-acre house lots. Of course Phil and Doug were both golfers, and this made a good beginning.

But what was put together by foresight and patience and fortitude, was the imaginative combination of elements

59

described in last Friday's Gazette, with Charles H. Harff, L. Robert Fullem and Douglass Mabee as general partners. Felix Neck gets 85 acres of a critically important region, long sought through years of suspense, as a gift. For open space, 265 acres reaching down to Sengekontacket Pond will be preserved always, with 48 well-sited two-acre house lots in a limited development economically supporting the whole. A covenant assures five acres of youth lots to be administered by the Vineyard Open Land Foundation.

Of the golf course, Mr. Harff says that when it matures "in a few years, it will be one of the best courses in New England. It's an interesting, tough and scenically exquisite course,"

What more? An architectural review committee will approve building designs, scenic views are protected, the cutting of trees and shrubbery is regulated.

All this is not local to Sengekontacket or Felix Neck or Oak Bluffs, but of critical regional importance to Martha's Vineyard as an Island community, famous for its variety, yet owning in the long run a single identity and treasury of natural resources including sky, earth, ponds and sea."

———————————————————————

Three: DESIGNING AND BUILDING THE GOLF COURSE

While the Strocks were endeavoring to obtain approval of their development plan, Island Properties built the first nine holes of the new golf course. It was designed by Geoffrey Cornish and William Robinson who made excellent use of the natural topography. The course work was done by Steve and Tony Paganis, experienced golf course contractors who had built courses around the United States as well as Canada and Nova Scotia. For example, the top of the sand pit that was below the 3rd tee provided an excellent elevation from which Sengekontacket Pond and Chappaquidick could be seen once trees were cleared; and moreover the sand pit provided an opportunity for the many traps that grace the fairway on that hole.

Similarly, the salt marshes that intersect the 8th fairway provided challenges for golfers on their tee shots, while Sengekontacket Pond on the right was not only visually most attractive, but also provided a major problem for any errant sliced tee shot. Cornish and Robinson's initial design of the 8th hole contemplated that it would be the signature hole for the golf course.

The championship tee was to be some 50 yards behind the current championship tee and the green was designed to be at the point across the northeast part of the Pond, reachable for golfers by a small cable-ferryboat, where there currently is a dock jutting out into the water. The initial design also contemplated that the tee for the 9th hole would be near that planned 8th green, about where the osprey pole now stands, thus requiring a nearly 200 yard drive across the marsh to a landing area on the way to the 9th green. Had that part of the golf course design ever been completed, it would have been a challenge for even the best golfers and certainly not friendly to the average golfer who now so much enjoys Farm Neck. In any event, for 1979 only these nine holes were available for play at Farm Neck.

Formal Subdivision Plan

The hard work of implementing the rest of the golf course and development plan began immediately after completion of the purchase. Rob Kendall, who had served as a consultant to the Open Land Foundation, was retained to develop definitive plans for the subdivision and Tim Sweet, who had worked for Island Properties since the mid-1960's, was appointed General Manager for the project. These were two of the best decisions made in the early stages of development. As reported in a letter of October 23, 1978, sent to each of the participants in the Farm Neck purchase:

———————————————————————

"Congratulations! The Farm Neck purchase closed on Friday, October 20, so that Farm Neck Associates now owns all of the former Strock properties known as Waterview III, IV and VI, comprising approximately 550 acres, with the exception of the motel.

The closing on the motel did not take place on the 20th. We, however, assigned the agreement we had with Deljavin Corp. to Bass River, and Bass River gave the Deljavin group until November 30 to complete its purchase. The motel property, which the Bank retains, comprises only 6.8 acres.

You will be interested to know that Rob Kendall has been working since the first of October on definitive plans for the subdivision. We are hopeful that a subdivision plan can be submitted to the Oak Bluffs Planning Board and the Martha's Vineyard Commission by the end of December or in the early part of January. Pat Mulligan has spent several days on the Vineyard this month working on the plans for the additional nine holes of the golf course, and an extended meeting regarding the golf course plans has already also taken place. Finally, Tim Sweet has been working for us also since the beginning of October in attending to the many necessary details."

───────────────────

Our belief that the Commission and Planning Board would approve our plans turned out to be correct as both bodies approved the subdivision plan in February 1979. In its January 17, 1979 edition *The Grapevine* reported:

───────────────────

"The Martha's Vineyard Commission (MVC) will almost certainly approve the preliminary plan for a 411-acre 51-residential lot subdivision to be located on the west end of Sengekontacket Pond for which a Development of Regional Impact (DRI) hearing was held last Thursday. The plan includes a public golf course and a substantial amount of open space to make it an appealing proposal for even the most conservative commissioners. It is inevitably compared to the far denser plan for the same property stymied by a Massachusetts Supreme Judicial Court decision last year.

Aerial view (about 1976) of the 8th fairway and green. The point at the left is where the 8th green was initially planned to be.

The new proposal submitted by Farm Neck Associates, was planned with the cooperation of Robert Kendall of the Vineyard Open Land Foundation. Kendall presented details of the plan at the heavily attended hearing.

The golf course would cover about half the area of the subdivision and would extend the nine-hole course presently on the property to the full 18 holes. A system of foot or horse paths weave through the area. Lot sizes are from 1.6 to 3.6 acres. Larger than Oak Bluffs zoning regulations call for. A homeowners' association will be established to review architectural plans for new houses.

Craig Kingsbury figured that the high-priced houses that will be built in the subdivision will bring in a large amount of revenue to the town and much more than the property now affords. He thought it was a 'good deal.' MVC chairperson Benjamin Moore commended the sensitivity of the plan and its concern for the environment."

Design of New Back Nine

Patrick S. Mulligan, the golf course designer selected to complete the back nine holes of the proposed golf course, in his letter of October 27, 1978 raised a number of preliminary questions which simply show the myriad of details that had to be dealt with expeditiously. Illustratively, he asked whether there were plans and specifications for an irrigation system on the front nine, whether anything had already been planned for the back nine, what is the capacity of the well and do we know peak volumes as well as the quality of the water; is it possible to muffle the engine for the wells without compromising either power or the irrigation program; is there a quality mechanic who could maintain the golf course equipment, and whether it would require bringing existing equipment up to first class condition; what equipment was there available or could be acquired at reasonable cost for mowing fairways, greens and tees, raking traps, spreading fertilizer, etc.; what is the size of the staff needed to maintain the golf course and how experienced is our greens keeper? It should be noted that the greens keeper, Mike Alwardt, has been with Farm Neck from its very beginning and, while relatively "green" when Farm Neck began, has grown over the 25 years he has so ably served, becoming one of the finest golf course superintendents and greens keepers anywhere. Pat Mulligan's design concept was focused on creating for the back nine a Scottish-type course.

As he noted in an article co-authored with John Williams McGrath for the Urban Land Institute: [6]

"Historically, golf came from penny-wise, pound-wise Scotland. A review of the traditional great golf courses and golf's evolution, evidences the pragmatic roots of golf which ensured its survival. The length of courses and individual holes, the sequence of pars, the types of holes, the extent of artificial hazards, of earth moving, of landscaping, and grooming, and the size of tees and greens for holes reflected the limitations of the times, the site, and the construction budget – often with little or no effect on the quality of play. Consistent with these extremely practical origins of golf, there are many current design concepts (some of which have become almost sacred)

which can be violated, while in no way compromising golf as a game of tradition and enjoyment."

———————————

Thus it should have been no surprise that the new back nine had relatively narrow fairways with high roughs ready to make any errant shot most difficult. As the course matured over the next 25 years, partly in response to the frustrations of golfers finding themselves in knee-high rough and partly in an effort to help meet Farm Neck's desire for four-hour rounds of golf, the fairways became wider and a much shorter intermediate rough made Farm Neck somewhat less like Scottish courses graced by insurmountable obstacles of gorse and knee- if not waist-high rough.

Pat Mulligan's thoughts about development of the golf course expressed a clear understanding of the importance of assuring an environmentally sensitive golf course while concurrently focusing on the economics of the proposed development. In his memorandum of February 6, 1979, he noted:

———————————

"...the golf design must:" (among other things)
- *be sensitive to Sengekontacket Pond's ecosystem*
- *take note of the natural drama of the site itself as well as of the adjacent Pond and Nantucket Sound*
- *be of championship caliber for marketing*
- *play enjoyably for all, independent of handicap*
- *provide for public play*
- *be fun"*

———————————

At the same time Pat was not totally prescient, for he added:

———————————————————

"Any golf program for Farm Neck must appreciate that the demonstrable Vineyard golf market does not financially sustain the Island's presently operating golf facilities. All criteria for planning, design, constructing, maintaining, marketing, owning and operating this proposed golf program should keep market expansion (creation) uppermost."

———————————————————

His overview comments on the challenges and ambience for the second nine holes are worth recalling:

———————————————————

"The world's greatest golf courses are recognized as such primarily as a result of the natural beauty and drama present on site before golf. First the designer should do no harm.

Scale is a constant issue. The roll and movement of this land against the sea creates long and subtle views, easily violated. Golfing features should frame and accent, not compete. Vegetation is generally low in profile and should not be compromised by huge golfing features.

The existing nine has a woodsy & closed feel. The new nine has an opportunity for a meadow-y or open impression. These pastures are reminiscent of golf's original courses still played in the British Isles. The LINKS [Farm Neck was initially named 'The Links at Martha's Vineyard,' a name that early on was replaced] will attempt to capture the emotion of historical golf while accommodating contemporary maintenance economies as well as modern golf equipment and skills.

The eco balance of Sengekontacket Pond is most delicate and cherished. Chemically laced runoff from the golf course must be diverted even during construction away from the Pond and allowed to percolate, thus eliminating any adverse effects. (Thank God the site is sandy). Drainage will be most carefully studied and managed.

Ground water in certain low spots is exposed & breeds mosquitoes; control of these pests improves the playing experience as well as provides some justification for the creation of some ponds, and the opportunity for the designer to keep at least one of his employers happy.

Obviously views to the water are most desirable. But, in addition, the site features some unique situations, such as the kettle holes which have been designed into play on #13 and the wet depressions designed into play on #12.

With the pastoral nature to the site for the new nine some attempt at capitalizing on this aspect as a theme should be evaluated. Historically golf was routed through farmland and felt like it. There are several locations in the present routing which could provide a setting for this theme to be punctuated."

More specifically, Pat Mulligan's proposal included a discussion of the type of golf course he had in mind in designing the new back nine:

————————————————

"The LINKS NEW NINE is a par 37 of championship length & quality. The golf course is safe for players, property owners, and passers-by. All target areas are visible — no blind shots.

The LINKS is designed to provided a 'MARTHA'S VINEYARD GOLF EXPERIENCE.' The LINKS will be
- enjoyable;
- beautiful in modest profile;
- a first class golfing challenge;
- to all golfers, Yankee in mood: tough, almost stingy, but fair;
- economic in the classic Yankee manner;
- exceptional, for once exposed the heathen must be immediately converted;
- respectful of the origins of golf and emulate fine historical experiences ala Scottish & Irish courses.

Since the new nine is designed with four sets of tees to accommodate a variety of play and players, any golfer who exercises his or her tee options honestly will face a golfing challenge second to none for no hole can be 'beaten.' Each hole may be tough, even unrelenting, but for the patient and confident, rewarding.

Whatever a golfer's handicap THE LINKS will test his or her game to their particular skill limit. At no time will a golfer feel penalized unjustly. 'A fine shot will find an even finer line, in line.' And by the end of a round each golfer will be more than casually acquainted with all his clubs.

The front plays short; the back, though long, can play as short as the front.

The key to this course is control, after careful club selection. Despite the length, finesse will win."

Building New Course

The winter of 1978 was a busy time indeed as design concepts for the golf course, master planning the definitive site locations, identifying potential areas for roads and utilities, and considering potential areas for either outright donation or environmental easements and restrictions began. Over the summer of 1979, construction of the new back nine started, with earth moving (modest in deference to the wonderful terrain and our limited budget), tree clearing, irrigation, sand traps and all the other aspects of a course beginning to take shape.

Tony Paganis, who had built the first nine, returned with great enthusiasm to work on the second nine. Not only had he taken a loss from his earlier work as Island Properties declared bankruptcy, but much to his credit and to Farm Neck's limited resources, he did the work on the new nine at the same price he had quoted initially several years earlier when doing the first nine. This was an important factor in helping to meet the limited budget for the new back nine. Pat Mulligan, in the design of the new nine, was very conscious of the fiscal restraints that only provided a budget of $250,000 for building the new nine. Even in 1979, a number of courses spent nearly that much on one hole and sometimes on only one or two greens. Were it not for careful use of the existing contours of the land, the relative ease of working in sandy rather than rocky soil, and most importantly the resources brought to bear by Farm Neck's greens' keeper, Mike Alwardt, and his crew who performed a good deal of the work necessary to build the new nine, the costs could easily have been more than doubled.

Doug also described what he considered the gamble in the project:

————————————————————

"The "Links" was to be a natural golf course with minimum maintenance. Little earth moving was involved except for the greens and tees. The fairways were to 'go with the flow' —

scale important — take advantage of the glacier 'kettle holes' — preservation of the eco balance of the Pond by 'berming' to allow percolation and diversion of chemicals — minimum use of traps etc, etc — These were some of the criteria. Great, but 'how the hell do you think the Vineyard can support an 18-hole 'championship' course when Mink Meadows is practically defunct? No players will be attracted from Edgartown — that course serves its purpose beautifully. One can play nine holes, pull his own cart, and finish in time to get on the courts or be ready for the afternoon Yacht Club races. Well, the truth of the matter was we did not know. It was a gamble that really couldn't even be classified as a calculated risk.

People didn't come to the Vineyard to play golf — that was a known fact. The Island presented too many attractions, or distractions, of another sort.

If this baby doesn't fly, we're going to be left with some of the most expensive (irrigated) farmland on the Island. No doubt about that. Said in jest but too close to the mark to be a laughing matter. Our deed, in essence, prohibited any other use except for agriculture. Fantasy or folly? Time would tell."

———————————————

The *Vineyard Gazette* in its June 29, 1979 edition reported extensively on the Island's new and only 18-hole course in an article entitled "Farm Neck Links Are Now Adding Back Nine Holes":

———————————————

"Soon Martha's Vineyard will have its own 18-hole, championship quality golf course at Farm Neck in Oak Bluffs. There are nine holes now in play at the site, and by the beginning of next year's golfing season the second nine will be complete.

Construction and planning of the second nine holes, which span more than 60 acres of land, has already begun, and according to course designer Patrick S. Mulligan, it should be completed by mid-September. The landscaping will be given a chance to take hold during the fall and spring with the new grasses ready for play by June 1980.

All the organizers of the project admit the substantial financial risk involved in building a golf course of this caliber on the Island. They expect that with a modest fee schedule and sensitive management the Farm Neck course could do very well.

Timothy Sweet of Farm Neck Associates says that with an increase in the amount of organized recreation on Martha's Vineyard and the realization that there is good golfing available, the club should be economically viable.

'The people who first set up the association wanted to find an economically feasible way to save the property without raping it,' said Mr. Sweet. 'I think they've found it in the combination of the 50 lots and the 18-hole golf course.'

'The community really has to identify itself with the course,' says Mr. Mulligan. 'We want to be able to seduce the avid golfer who now spends all of his time on the Vineyard sailing, but golfs all winter long in Florida. The aim is to give the golfers the length and challenge they are used to without building anything that's offensive to the

Vineyard. It's really going to be a Vineyard golf course.'

Representatives of Farm Neck Associates and Mr. Mulligan stress the fact that the course is being designed in such a way as to make optimum use of the existing landscape, and to conserve the special feeling of the Island.

The Oak Bluffs Conservation Commission met last night to consider the club's plans to change some low-lying marsh areas into small ponds. The plans are designed to rid the area of some bad mosquito breeding grounds; Mr. Mulligan expects that the changes will enhance the wildlife in the area rather than disturb it.

The hazards to be set up around the course will use natural meadows seeded with Island wildflowers instead of the usual sand traps and water obstacles that are found in golf courses in Florida or California. The designer's intention is to make the most of the visual effects of the Island landscape.

Another concern of Mr. Mulligan's in designing the course is to keep the safety standards at a maximum. Although part of the course borders on Beach Road and will surround a number of houses, Mr. Mulligan says that it will be very safe because of the distances he has allowed in laying it out.

The cost of construction of the new nine holes may be as much as $400,000, but with the high quality of the course Mr. Mulligan says it will be easy and inexpensive to maintain over the years.

'The course compares very well with off-Island courses,' said Mr. Mulligan. 'I'd say that even players like Tom Watson and Jack Nicklaus would be challenged by it. It's unique because of its adherence to the Vineyard landscape patterns. You'll be playing the Vineyard, not just a golf course.'"

———————————————

In a letter from Doug Mabee, the first president of the Farm Neck Association dated July 15, 1980, he advised the members:

———————————————

"To everyone's amazement including my own, the back nine was opened for play to members of the Club July 3rd and to the public a day later. Amazement, because some of the greens and fairways were not seeded until November. A golf *course cannot be customized to everyone's ability – or taste. But now I think the Island golfing community has a course that offers incredible scenery, vistas and challenging play. Comment has been very favorable.*

Early May was plagued with cold, rainy weather and at times I thought it impossible that things could progress to the point we have finally reached. Mike Alwardt's original crew of three was gradually augmented to six; a full-time mechanic was added to keep the equipment in operating order and with untiring effort and planning by General Manager Tim Sweet, we made it."

Prophetically Doug's letter also noted,

"As play on the courts and golf course increase we foresee the need of a snack bar and lounge – with a few tables and chairs. We visualize something very modest immediately adjacent or connecting to the west side of the Pro Shop."

In writing to the members on November 20, 1980, Doug stated:

"Monday, November 3, was the end of a most successful season and our first as a full 18-hole course. We couldn't be more pleased with the enthusiastic reception the course has received from members and guests alike. We believe, now more than ever, that with several years of

maturity Farm Neck will become one of the truly outstanding golf courses in New England."

———————————

In his memoir recollections of the actual work of building the new nine holes, Doug noted:

———————————

"This was a labor of love for all of us but more especially for Mike Alwardt, who should be recognized as another (principal) contributor along with Tim and Rob. Mike was a three handicapper who gave up active play and winters in Florida to become course Superintendent. I have always felt it regrettable that Clubs, in general, do not give proper recognition to this position but if anything goes wrong ... brown spot, fungus, whatever, recognition comes quickly enough – for the wrong

reasons. Mike and his crew installed the entire irrigation systems, performed wonders with the 'tree spade' – a cone shaped hydraulic device used by nurserymen to dig and transplant trees, and had sustained the course during the lean Strock years when there was a shortage of funds for equipment, fertilizer, insecticides, water, you name it. He deserved the appointment."

———————————

In the Board's letter of July 15, 1981 to Farm Neck stockholders, the Board reported:

———————————

"The past year's been most successful for Farm Neck. As many of you who are on the Vineyard or visit frequently can attest, Farm Neck has made the transition from dream to reality. The golf course and tennis courts have *been completed and are operating well, the roads and utilities have long been finished and now seven houses are up or being built. Sense of community will not we are confident be far behind. Once again we urge all of you to become active members of the golf and tennis facilities and to encourage friends, too, to become charter members. For the first time, the Vineyard has a well-maintained, beautiful 18-hole championship golf course. Farm Neck's Har-Tru tennis courts may well be the finest on the Island. But to continue to maintain these facilities in first-class order requires a substantial budget. We are pleased to see revenues well ahead of last year, but 1981 will likely see an operating loss for the recreation facilities. Only full support of all of our property owners, and their sincere efforts to encourage friends to*

participate as members, will assure the long-term financial success of an obviously important aspect of Farm Neck."

———————————————————

Four: YEARS OF CHANGE AT FARM NECK

In his March 4, 1980 letter, Pat Mulligan urged that the ninth hole be changed as soon as possible noting, "My concern involves Hole No. 9 on the front loop at Farm Neck. At present it's a disaster as a Par 4, not worthy of the company it keeps; but as a Par 3 it creates a strong, exciting experience worthy of its company and a challenge to all." The first nine would then have three Par 3's and the back nine only one Par 3. Yet as Pat noted in the article he co-authored with John McGrath, [7]

"Design requires re-evaluation of the generally accepted notion that an 18-hole course should have the symmetry of two Par 3's on each nine and two Par 5's. …. "Sacred, although not taken quite as seriously, is the sequence of holes, e.g. no consecutive Par 3's or 5's; do not start or finish nine with a Par 3; each nine should contain two Par 3's and two Par 5's; each back nine should be balanced as to par and length; and so on…. Historical perspective seems to suggest these rules should be flexibly applied. In the Top Ten Tests of Golf in the United States (Golf Digest 1974), we find the front nines of Marion (East), Oakland Hills and Pinehurst No. 2 all close with a Par 3."

He also refers to other famous courses such as Baltusrol, Winged Foot, Cherry Hills and the Country Club as fine courses that violate "the accepted theories of golf course design." He also noted that changing the 9th to a Par 3 would result in a Par 71 course rather than the traditional Par 72, but that was perfectly acceptable, particularly since 25% of the top 20 courses according to Golf Digest also are

View from the 8th hole of Sengekontacket Pond and bordering marshland.

Par 71. This would not become an issue for Farm Neck for the 8th hole was lengthened to become a Par 5 concurrent with the change to the 9th, thus retaining a Par 72 course.

Reactions to the new course, generally enthusiastic, were prompt and occasionally a bit frustrated. In a letter of July 22, 1980 to Pat Mulligan, I said

---

"Now that we have had three weeks of play on the new nine, the howls about the difficulty about some of the rough are abating somewhat, although I'm sure we have gone a little further than you would approve in cutting some of the rough near the fairways in an effort to speed up play. Your observation that the course seems longer than it really plays couldn't be more correct, although in part that is a reflection of location of tee markers, which in the first few weeks have been further forward than Bob and I would like to see them in time to come. No one, for example has tried the back tees on the 18th – from the intermediate (white tee), it actually is a very fair par which can be reached with a fairly easy short iron on the third shot (assuming you stayed out of the marsh or meadow, no small feat indeed). Similarly, the 12th, which continues to be my special favorite, is nowhere near as difficult as I had thought; particularly if the drive is sent way over to the right rather than down the fairway...but that sort of play recognizes a certain gambler's willingness to go into the woods if the shot is not correctly played...it will be interesting to see how the course develops as it matures. In the meantime, I know I speak for all of us in complimenting you for your dedicated and successful effort."

Family of Canadian Geese on the 15th green.

YEARS OF CHANGE AT FARM NECK

Course Improvements

Changes did not come quickly at Farm Neck, not because the founders were unaware of a number of potential improvements, but because the driving mantra for Farm Neck always was to live within its means. The stockholders who comprised the initial participants in the Strock Property purchase funded the Farm Neck Golf Course with sufficient monies to acquire all the equipment initially required and provided approximately $100,000 to assure Farm Neck's viability in the early years. Nevertheless operating losses, together with the slow addition to membership, led to Farm Neck's first and only borrowing early in 1981. A short-term loan of $25,000 was arranged with Bass River Savings Bank and promptly repaid later that year on completion of the sale of one of the two farmhouses on the property.

Improvements to the golf course were only made as Farm Neck's annual cash flow improved and changes could be funded from annual revenues. As originally intended, Farm Neck has been and intends always to be a not-for-profit enterprise, with whatever annual profits it has to be plowed back into course improvements and a continuing effort to keep member fees as low as possible consistent with maintaining a first-rate facility.

One of the earliest changes was increasing the number of golf carts. Unlike many new courses, Farm Neck was designed to be a "walking course". Nevertheless, we soon learned that there was more demand for carts than we had anticipated. We started with a fleet of ten that became 20 early in the 1980's and year by year grew to 60. In response to member requests, by 1995 all carts also had windscreens

View of the 15th hole after the pond in front of the green was enlarged and extended to the right side.

and roofs. The ever-expanding cart fleet also saw the original cart paths of wood chips replaced, to the chagrin of those who liked their rustic look, little by little with asphalt. Aesthetically, however, we tried as much as possible to hide the cart paths among trees lining the fairways. The 1993 annual members report noted, that we will hard top those paths most used and stated:

"Good or bad, golf carts have become an integral part of the game of golf. Because the visual aesthetics of Farm Neck are of such importance to us, we have been reluctant in the past to pursue a permanent solution to deteriorating cart paths on the course."

In response to member comments, the fairways were widened somewhat, particularly on the new back nine, and the rough was trimmed as well – "improvements" that were not costly and helped in Farm Neck's never ending quest for four-hour rounds. In a letter of September 12, 1982 to Messrs. Fullem, Harff and Mabee, a resident of West Chop wrote: "My wife and I have enjoyed very much playing Farm Neck this summer. It is a real challenge and an interesting course with beautiful views. From tee to green it has been in excellent shape. The green's keeper is to be complimented. The staff in the Clubhouse is pleasant, polite and helpful. All handle their jobs with good humor and a smile." He added several suggestions, including... "the 'playable' rough adjacent to the fairways should be widened and the abominable 'high' rough (from a golfer's point of view) outside of that should be cut so that there is a reasonable

Fall foliage across the pond on the 12th hole.

chance of finding balls when you make a shot.' As of now, it is almost impossible to do either."

One of the more dramatic changes was made in 1985 on the 15th hole as the pond, rather than being only in front of the 15th green, was enlarged to run parallel with the green.

The hole was made even more difficult in 1996 when a new series of tees was built and the green became a two-tiered green with the front part closer to the water's edge; but at the same time a trap was added to the right of the green to stop reasonably well hit balls from rolling into the water. In 1986 the pond in front of the 9th hole was also enlarged to promote added challenge for long-ball hitters who tried to reach the green on their tee shots (this was before the 9th was changed to a Par 3).

Additional changes were made in 1986, included enlarging the pond on the 12th to eliminate standing water problems in the landing area, enlarging the tees on 4, 5, 7 and 8, doubling the size of the club storage building that had only been built a couple of years earlier, and building a new tennis pro shop.

In 1987 and 1988, further improvements to the tees on the front nine were made, new bunkers were added on 10, 14 and 16 and the fairway bunkers on 16 were eliminated, together with several trees in the center of the fairway that while scenic were not a proper course hazard. A program to over-seed the fairways with bent grass was also started as the Club found the original blue grass could not tolerate the increasing volume of golf cart traffic.

Recent view of driving range with multiple sandtraps and target greens.

By our tenth anniversary in 1989, we made a few modest changes. To the left side of the fairway on the 6th hole the first of many new ladies' tees was added; and a new 10,000 square foot putting green built in the previous year adjacent to the 10th tee was ready for play. A large oak tree to the left of the 11th was replaced by several bunkers so as to improve the health of the green. On the 13th new bunkers were added to guard the approach to the green.

As Bob Fullem noted in the 1990 annual report, "The putting green and practice range are a very important, though often forgotten, part of any golf club. With the opening of the new putting green last year, we completed the first half of upgrading our practice areas. This year we will concentrate on improving our driving range." While it was doubled in size and lengthened 50 yards, with a couple of target greens and a new teaching tee, it and the putting greens were only the first of the changes that over time greatly further enhanced the Club's practice facilities.

Over the past years there have been continuing changes to the practice areas. When the course opened in 1979, the only putting green was the one in front of the Pro Shop. (This relic from the early days was eliminated in 2004 when the starter's gazebo was moved to this newly landscaped area.) One by one there was added first the practice green near the 10th tee, with this practice area expanded in 1995 to include two putting greens, a chipping green and bunkers for sand trap practice. The driving range was relocated several times and in 2001 was significantly enlarged and re-sculpted so that it now may well be the most expansive and best driving range in the United States. As part of that project, an additional putting green was added near the driving range and a much larger teaching tee was also provided.

During the fall and winter our invaluable grounds crew cleaned up from the 1991 Hurricane Bob that destroyed over 1,000 trees on Farm Neck. This they did so well that the loss of so many trees was hardly noticeable when play resumed in 1992. Also in 1992 new championship tees were added on 16 and 18 and ladies' tees on 5, 8 and 9 were either improved or relocated.

The pace of change had heightened appreciably in 1992. In the interests of keeping down the costs of building the new nine, many compromises had to be made in 1979. For example

the gully in front of the 16th tee from the very beginning looked as if it should be filled with water. Yet that excellent addition, which substantially altered and improved both the 16th and 17th holes, would not take place for 13 years. As reported in the 1992 annual report to members:

"We have undertaken our most ambitious golf course renovation project thus far at Farm Neck. We are now totally renovating the 17th hole. This renovation includes exciting changes not only to 17, but 16 and 18 as well."

A pond of approximately one-and-a-half acres was created in front of the 16th tee and close to the edge of the new 17th. The 1992 report added:

"The new hole will play a slight dog-leg over the pond with a water carry similar to the 7th on your second shot. The less venturesome will find an alternative fairway approach, with strategically placed traps, instead of going over the pond."

Pat Mulligan's early identification of the need to change the 9th hole to a Par 3 did not occur until 1993 when concurrently the 8th hole was lengthened from a 401-yard Par 4 to a 504-yard Par 5 by moving the green to the edge of the marsh near where the tee for the 9th hole had been, and building new tees on the hillside to make the 9th hole into a par 3. It was also at this time that the double green for the 9th and 18th was split and the pond in front of these

holes re-contoured so that part of it would come closer to the 9th green. In the 1993 annual members' report, I noted:

"Flush with success from last year's renovation of the sixteenth and seventeenth holes, last October we began another major improvement to the golf course. This time on the front nine. After years of unsuccessfully trying to twist, turn and cajole the ninth hole into a legitimate Par 4, we have taken the totally new approach to the problem...we decided to create a superior par 3."

The 1993 report also commented on Farm Neck's continued sensitivity to its founding spirit of maintaining the beauty and environment of this important Vineyard area:

───────────────────────────────

"Last year as part of our continuing commitment to the preservation and protection of Farm Neck's property and environment, we joined the Audobon Cooperative Sanctuary Program. This innovative program by the Audobon Society was created to work with golf courses on an international basis to promote ecological consciousness on their increasingly important tracts of undeveloped land. One part of the program is to promote and provide nesting areas in the open habitat of golf courses. Farm Neck is blessed with a unique combination of open fields, woodlands, marshlands and bodies of fresh and salt water which make it particularly attractive to a wide variety of birds. After consulting with Felix Neck, last spring we began the first phase of constructing nesting sites throughout the property. In

addition to the osprey pole we erected four years ago, we added two wood duck boxes, 24 tree swallow boxes and one barn owl house. Over the next several years we plan to continue to expand the number and types of nesting areas."

───────────────────────────────

Of course no change at Farm Neck remains static. Thus the 17th green was re-contoured and made 25% larger in 1996, with all its sub-soil replaced, in the never-ending quest to seek improvements. For those who have been members for much of the Club's 25-year history, they will remember the problems posed by a large pine tree at the dogleg corner of the 11th hole. With great consternation among many, in 1996 the tree was removed and replaced by several sand traps. Notwithstanding the initial dismay about this change, there developed clear unanimity relatively soon that the tree had not been an asset. In fact the traps were a more fair impediment.

In 1997, the 10th hole was lengthened some 60 yards, with traps protecting it on both the right and left to assure that it would be a more challenging hole than its original design (once again, nothing remains static, for the left hand pot bunker only remained a couple of years before becoming a shallower grass area). Four new tees were added to give the 10th hole a different perspective, following the same type of change made on the 11th hole when trees were cleared so the tees could be moved further to the left and a field of wild flowers could replace the former tees to enhance the beauty of that hole.

In 1998, the 13th hole was changed dramatically by building a new elevated, more contoured green further to the south and guarding it with new traps on both the left and right sides. Moreover, the fairway was re-contoured with additional traps while new elevated tee boxes were also added. At the same time, new tees were built on the 14th hole and the play directed further away from Beach Road.

In 1999 we finally lost the very large beautiful old oak tree that protected the dogleg on the 12th hole. After one season of playing that hole without this important impediment, it became clear that the tree had to be replaced. The first effort in 2001 failed, but a second replacement the following year is prospering and hopefully will in time grow to be as big as the wonderful tree that was an important feature in the initial design of the 12th hole.

Without going into further hole-by-hole recollections, substantially all the tees have been either renovated or moved so that there are now four tees on each hole with an approximately 500 yard course length difference between each of the four tees. Moreover, as more and more ladies began to play golf, the forward tees were increased in size and the locations changed significantly. In addition, trees were moved or eliminated from time to time to improve playability of the course.

Of course there are many, many other changes, including moving or redesigning a number of sand traps and importing (hard to believe on an island with so many beaches) quality sand from off-Island to replace the original Island sand, and planting a number of trees around the course, either to provide definition or, as in the case of the area between 16 and 17, to provide greater separation. In 1998, Farm Neck also joined the growing number of courses to require soft spikes and thus help assure the greens are as playable near the end of the day as at the beginning.

New Buildings

While all these changes were made over time on the golf course, the physical plant was changed dramatically from 1979 when only a small pro shop was available. Year by year, in perfect site planning and architectural cohesiveness, Tim Sweet's edifice complex came to the fore. First a small snack bar was built across from the Pro Shop, only to be expanded through several iterations as snacks gave way to a Café for breakfast, lunch and then dinner service. In addition, a large flat space was created next to the Café for a tented area for large club events, weddings and private parties.

The Pro Shop was also enlarged several times with accompanying increases in inventory of golf equipment and clothing. A locker and club storage facility was added early on and then expanded as the membership grew. Similarly the Club's office, which initially was in a barn adjacent to one of the farm houses that had been part of the Strock properties, was relocated to a new office building that too was expanded several times as Farm Neck's staff increased with the added requirements of an ever-growing membership. The last addition (at least for the first 25 years) was a new members' locker room building, replete with men's and ladies' showers. Over time the golf cart storage facilities were revamped and enlarged repeatedly. The maintenance buildings, too, were renovated and enlarged as the increasing demands for more and better machinery made it imperative to assure that necessary equipment would be properly stored and well maintained.

In the tennis area a new Pro Shop was built and several years later expanded to provide more appropriate space for the display and sale of tennis equipment and clothing. Moreover, to facilitate tournament play, a viewing stand was built and the area around the court was enhanced by a signature gazebo and lots of distinctive plantings. One of our first board members, Phil Brown, was the Board's primary overseer of the tennis program and facilities. Sadly, Phil died too soon and in our 1997 members report we noted:

_____

"*Sadly, mixed with all our improvements, Farm Neck suffered a great loss this fall with the passing of Phil Brown. Phil was a founding member of the Farm Neck Board of Directors in 1979. His love of the games of golf and, especially, tennis was infectious. His generosity of time, spirit and counsel was invaluable in helping bring shape and substance to the vision of Farm Neck."*

———————————————————

A plaque in his honor is installed in the tennis gazebo.

Tim Sweet's sense of aesthetics and pride helped create a particular Farm Neck ambience. The Club's signage is distinctive; its plantings and flowers are lovely, yet in keeping with the character of Farm Neck, with abundant wild flowers in a number of strategic locations; and the parking lot, which so often at other clubs is prosaic at best, has been attractively designed with much stone work and many small islands assuring that it is distinctive and uniquely different than a conventional parking lot. A tribute must be paid to Sara Alwardt who for most of Farm Neck's existence has done wonders in maintaining the flower

beds around the course, first by herself and then, as more and larger flower beds have been added, with expert help as the number of gardeners has increased over the years.

Sara Alwardt in front of one of the many lovely flower beds.

A Work In Progress

For those who've seen Farm Neck mature gradually over its first 25 years, the transformation is startling indeed. When Farm Neck opened in 1979 it was the culmination of a dream. Yet we never envisioned that it would become so vastly much better.

In the 10th anniversary member booklet, the President's letter stated:

———————————————

"Looking back it is hard to believe that it has already been ten years and, at the same time, it is often difficult to remember a time when Farm Neck wasn't here. Ten years ago who would have believed that Martha's Vineyard would now be equated with great golf or that players would be comparing Farm Neck to the best courses they have ever played. In the beginning our goal was not so much to be thriving in ten years, but to just still be here.

Unquestionably, we've had some great luck and good timing but through all these years we've had one real constant, an incredibly dedicated staff. They could have easily put in their time and just maintained the status quo during these past years. Luckily they have never been satisfied with adequate. Their continuous efforts to ever improve Farm Neck, year in and year out, is why we have what we have today. We all share in their pride and thank them for their dedication in our behalf."

———————————————

The 1995 members' booklet stated:

"We are again gratified to see that, in the eyes of most members and public players, the Club has continued to improve in just about all areas. Ironically, however, the Club's continued improvement has also become a major area of concern, for as one member responded [in the third edition of the Club's every-five year members' survey], 'It must be very frustrating to be a victim of the pursuit of excellence. Having guys like me constantly wanting everything bigger and better, and at the same time, insisting that dues and fees remain low, and then, after you've accomplished the impossible, complaining that you've done such a good job that we can't get on the course any more.'"

In reminiscing about the origins of Farm Neck in the annual members' booklet commemorating the 20th anniversary of Farm Neck, we reminded ourselves of the origins of Farm Neck:

"In the mid-1970's, what is now Farm Neck nearly became a development of over 800 house sites on quarter acre lots. When that developer failed, we envisioned instead, a golf course designed with as few house sites as would permit a debt-free purchase of the property and allow for creation of a not-for-profit golf club. From its inception we have had two basic guiding principles; a commitment to excellence and an effort to create a non-exclusive golf course accessible to as broad a range of Vineyard residents and visitors as possible. The skepticism that greeted this concept was demonstrated by the fact that it took over

eight years to reach our modest goal of 150 Charter Members. The widely held view at the time was that Farm Neck would most certainly fail. Fail we did not.

Ironically and in sharp contrast to our early years, Farm Neck has so grown in popularity that trying to equitably serve all those who wish to enjoy our facilities has become our greatest challenge. Under different leadership, this problem could be easily resolved by either becoming a private club with limited membership, or by following the tried and true laws of supply and demand and rocketing our rates upward. Neither of these alternatives, however, is what Farm Neck is all about."

Mike Alwardt, Golf Course Superintendent (on right) and John Holenko, Assistant Superintendent.

Fred Sonnenberg, Club Engineer and his assistant.

Nothing has changed, for Farm Neck continues to improve year in and year out and the dedication of the staff and its allegiance to Farm Neck have never wavered. The golf course has changed year by year as the resources needed for improvement have become available. The many changes over the years have been made significantly better and more affordable as time and again we relied on the dedicated, professional efforts of Mike Alwardt and his crew, always aided and abetted by the skilled talents of our long-time Club Engineer, Fred Sonnenberg. Fred, who had enjoyed a long career as an engineer, "retired" to the Vineyard just in time to spend over fifteen years assuring Farm Neck's maintenance equipment and irrigation systems have always been in "Apple Pie" order.

Five: FARM NECK MEMBERSHIP

While the success in rescuing the 500+ acres abutting Sengekontacket from overdevelopment received a good deal of recognition, golfers did not immediately clamor to join as members. The initiation fee for charter memberships, which were limited to 150, was $750 for the first fifty charter members, $1,000 for the next fifty and $1,500 for the last fifty. The annual dues initially were $250. Special Island memberships were also offered to Island registered voters with no initiation fees and dues of $50 per year to be supplemented by greens fees of $2.50 per round, available only in off-peak periods.

Even after the new nine holes were completed, golfers still were not clamoring to join. While Farm Neck was then the only 18-hole course on Martha's Vineyard, this was still a time when the Vineyard's attraction was more "sun, sea and sand" and perhaps tennis, but golf was more likely considered a distraction from family vacations.

Notwithstanding the excellence of the golf course even in its early years, membership grew slowly. Partly this reflected a significant concern among many on the Vineyard that Farm Neck was doomed to fail and that joining would simply be a waste of money. Others had different reasons as noted in a letter dated September 10, 1981 to Doug Mabee:

_____

"John and I have greatly enjoyed our membership at Farm Neck over the last two years. We find it a lovely and challenging course. As a result, we have encouraged friends in West Chop and Edgartown to join. Time and again the reaction has been the same. As members they *would pay more dues ($400 vs. the amount of green's fees they would pay for normal one month use plus initiation fee) and receive no real privileges. Basically these people are not concerned with the financial burden of membership, but can't justify membership vs. public play. We've been told by some that they intend to join when the Club gets close to filling its membership."*

———————————————

To help induce people to join, starting in 1980 the charter member initiation fee became fully refundable upon a member's decision to leave. The 150 charter memberships were not filled until 1986. At that time, a new category of "Full" membership was established with a non-refundable initiation fee of $1,500. The Board reserved the right to determine the number of full memberships to be offered

on a year-by-year basis. Several years later Farm Neck determined that the initiation fee with respect to all memberships should be made fully refundable so long as the total members remained no fewer. At its 25th Anniversary, Farm Neck has 284 stockholder, charter, full and associate members plus 136 Islander members.

The early initiation fees, annual dues and greens fees were a bargain, not only in relation to what they became over the years, but even in relation to comparable courses at that time. As costs escalated, and as the interest in membership increased, periodically the initiation fees and dues as well as greens fees for public and guest play increased. By 1996 the initiation fee had grown to $15,000, the annual dues to $1,200 and the Islander membership dues to $400. As was noted in the 1996 annual report to members:

"...we take great pride in the fact that Farm Neck's membership dues remain 1/2 to 1/4 the dues of comparable championship caliber Clubs. This remarkable difference in rates is possible for three simple reasons: (1) The decision of Farm Neck stockholders to operate a non-profit Club for the benefit of the Island rather than themselves, (2) the long-term loyalty and financial support of all the public players of Farm Neck, and (3) the steadfast dedication and accomplishments of Farm Neck's incredible staff. Without their collective contributions, which we often (regrettably) take for granted, Farm Neck would be a far different place today."

In 2003 a dramatic change was made in the initiation fee, with an increase from $25,000 to $100,000. Concurrently, the annual dues were increased to $1,400, continuing the Club's effort to maintain dues at an affordable level and far below those at comparable facilities. The initiation fee increase reflected the dramatic change in the market for golf on the Vineyard where even the increased initiation fee was far below that of the Island's recently created only other 18-hole golf course. Moreover, the change in the initiation fee (which continues to be refundable on the same basis as before the increase) was a major step in helping to maintain dues at a relatively low level. As was noted in the 2003 membership book:

"When you look back at the amazing transformation that has taken place at Farm Neck over the past twenty-four years, in the way of additions, renovations, improvements and refurbishment in almost every area of the Club, we're

proud that we've done it with extremely moderate dues and without a single assessment ever being charged to our membership."

———————————————

Leaving aside the historical recitation of Farm Neck's membership progress, the most memorable fact is that Farm Neck has remained true to its initial guiding principles which were:

- Golf in a resort community should be available to visitors and Island residents, and not exclusively to Club members.

- Membership and play should be affordable for year-round residents.

- Membership should be open to anyone regardless of race, creed, or economic or social status.

Farm Neck has prided itself on its heterogeneous membership, the result of its admissions policy of "first come, first admitted," with no admissions committee or impediments to membership other than the length of its waiting list (which of course did not begin to come into being until late in the 1980's). The fact that Farm Neck's tournaments, daily play and social events include a broad mixture of summer visitors, part-time Island residents and full-time Island members is a hallmark of Farm Neck that has given it a distinctive ambience.

Farm Neck's admissions policy, while it has served the Club well, came as a shock to some. One of the early inquiries regarding membership asked, "Who will be on your admissions committee and what are the membership criteria?" When advised that there would neither be a committee nor criteria, the puzzled individual asked, "But how can you be sure you will have the right people as members?" and was told, "We don't know who the 'right' people are, so as long as they enjoy golf they're welcome." Needless to say that individual did not join; but Farm Neck's "first come, first admitted" policy has stood the test of time. There is particular satisfaction in seeing year round Island businessmen, carpenters, builders, electricians and others sharing a golf tournament or play with CEOs of major companies, renowned government leaders, summer visiting teachers, doctors and lawyers, and retirees from all walks of life. Golf is, as it should be, the common denominator.

As on our 25th anniversary we look at our waiting list for full membership of 562 and for Island membership of 308, it appears that we have more than given people the impetus to join Farm Neck. Notwithstanding the length of our waiting list, we continue to believe that a semi-private course is far preferable, particularly in a resort community such as the Vineyard.

The spirit of Farm Neck is well captured in an article in the 2003 edition of Commonwealth Golf, which included:

———————————————————

"To understand Farm Neck, which was designed in 1976 by Geoffrey Cornish (only the front nine, as Pat Mulligan in 1979 designed the back nine)*, you've got to know the course's pro, Mike Zoll. If there was an award for nicest golf*

Mike Zoll, Head Golf Professional, at starter's gazebo.

pro in Massachusetts, it could very well go to Zoll. He came late to the business, going to the PGA school to get his professional teaching status (his 67 at Farm Neck tied Billy Andrade for the course record; it has since been broken). Share a coffee with Zoll, and you get a sense that this genial man would be happier playing the course, than running it. Over that coffee, you'll also get a sense of what golf means to those on the Vineyard, particularly public golf. 'The thing about Farm Neck,' says Zoll, 'is that it's open to everybody. We love the mix of the people and the income levels here. It creates freshness. The founders have never taken a penny out; they run it like a non-profit. Plus they set up a charitable foundation for nearby organizations.'"

Six: RECOGNITION

The history of Farm Neck would not be complete without a recitation of some of the many tributes it has received over the first quarter century of its existence. Farm Neck has been recognized as an outstanding golf course, with many accolades over the years. For example:

Business Week in its August 31, 1981 issue included Farm Neck among the *"best of the new golf courses"* along with the likes of Bear's Paw, TPC at Ponte Verde, La Quinta and Vintage.

The Boston Globe of August 20, 1989 included an article stating:

———————————————

"I consider Farm Neck one of the most beautiful natural golf courses in America...it is not the toughest course in the world, but it is challenging. When the wind blows it can give the best players fits. As one member put it, 'You never get bored waiting on a tee because there's always something beautiful to look at.' There are glimpses of rare birds nesting in the marshes as well as panoramic views of wind surfers off Nantucket Sound.

From the scoring pencils (with erasers) to the cans of bug spray at every tee, it is a special place. The score cards vary, with award winning photographs of the greens and holes. And there are unique local rules such as, 'Any ball moved or stolen by seagulls should be moved back or replaced at the original lie'."

———————————————

The July 1993 *Golf Digest* stated:

"Quite simply, this (Farm Neck) is about as good as a semi-private course is going to get. And the 34,000 rounds it saw last year is testimony to that, as are people coming over from the mainland just to play it. At 6,709 yards from the tips, Farm Neck is a stern, fair and really quite beautiful test of golf. It is carved through the woods, and water views are frequent and impressive."

The *Boston Globe* in its July 8, 1993 edition in designating its Hole of the Week stated:

"A jewel of a 12th graces Farm Neck." Adding, *"If you want to take a wonderful trip during the sizzling days of summer, take the ferry to Martha's Vineyard and play Farm Neck Golf Club. The hole you want to play and replay is the 12th...a Par is an excellent score."*

In the *Cape Cod Times Magazine* of October 8, 1993 it was reported that:

"The mainland has dozens of great golf courses, but you are cheating yourself if you don't make a trip to the Vineyard for a day at Farm Neck. Not just because this is where President Clinton played during his summer

vacation. The course, open to the public year-around, was always considered a hidden jewel. What makes the course so attractive from a purely golfing point of view, is its playability. For the high handicapper, there is room to miss shots and still recover."

In a letter to Farm Neck of December 4, 1995, *Par High Publishing* said:

"We would like to congratulate you on the selection of your golf course as a finalist to be included in the prestigious new book, 'American Golf Classics: 50 Courses Every Golfer Should (and Can!) Play.' The book will contain only the finest, most distinctive golf courses in

the United States that are either private or resort courses. This publication is intended to provide golfers of every age and playing ability an exciting reference guide of celebrated memorable golf courses that they should go out of their way to play in their lifetime."

The letter noted that Farm Neck had been selected out of over 500 courses. Others selected included such well-known courses as Bay Hill, Greenbriar, Kapalua, Doral, Harbor Town, Homestead, Spanish Bay, Pebble Beach, Sea Island, Mauna Kea and Spyglass.

The May/June 1997 edition of *Player – Magazine of U.S. Golf Society* stated:

———————————

"There's something about playing golf off the mainland – the air is cleaner and the colors more vivid. This (Farm Neck) is one of the most picturesque and challenging seaside courses in America."

———————————

In the September/October 1998 issue of *Senior Golfer* it was reported that:

———————————

"Geoffrey Cornish and Brian Silva, the undisputed kings of Cape Cod golf architecture designed a course located in the Vineyard town of Oak Bluffs. Farm Neck is a gem that nobody knew much about until President Clinton started playing golf there on his Vineyard summer vacations. Seven holes of the heavily bunkered Par 72, 6,777 yards of beauty are either played down to or along Nantucket Sound. And that is not the only water you'll see. The wet stuff comes into play on eight holes, including the final four. Although it's impossible to pick the most beautiful hole here, it is hard to top the 362 yard 3rd, which runs downhill toward the south; the 8th, a brutal 504 yard Par 5 that requires a 175 yard carry over a marsh to a fairway that runs alongside the Sound; or No. 14, a 339-yard dogleg left that features a green surrounded by a marsh and the Sound (sic Pond) on the right. Bring you're A-game and camera."

It adds:

"Farm Neck's Par 3 15th is a sight to behold despite the trouble" and "Even Farm Neck's tee signs are a thing of beauty."

———————————

By 2003, Farm Neck was clearly recognized as a leading course. It was included in the *Zagat Survey of American's Top Golf Courses*, ranking among the top three in New England. In its commentary Zagat noted:

"Yet another contender for the title of 'Pebble Beach of the East,' this 'superb' tract open April – December on Martha's Vineyard is a 'pleasure,' though with non-life members allowed to reserve only two days in advance, it's gotten closer to private than public; if you get on it you'll be playing a 'well-kept' course with 'endless character,' beautiful views of the Atlantic' and 'windy,' 'terrific risk/reward holes' that 'can bring golfers to their knees', which may explain why it's been the site of so 'many rounds by former President Clinton.'"

The 2003 *New England Golf Guide* listed it as a four-star course open for public play. *Travel and Leisure* in listing the best 50 golf courses in Massachusetts ranked Farm Neck as #2, while the *New England Journal of Golf* ranked it as #3 among the top 100 New England courses. The *Boston Magazine*, in ranking courses in Massachusetts open to the public, made Farm Neck #1, noting,

---

"This great Geoffrey Cornish creation on Martha's Vineyard is so good, many people make the trip across the water just to play it. There is nothing not to like from the shingled clubhouse to the expansive range to the glory of golf itself, especially the holes that border the adjacent bay."

View of the 17th hole, pond, and green.

Seven: COMMUNITY OUTREACH

As founders of Farm Neck we intended not only to provide the Vineyard with a first-rate golf course and to preserve a fragile and beautiful part of the Vineyard. We also sought to demonstrate a commitment to the spirit and sense of community of the Vineyard.

One of Farm Neck Associates' first charitable acts was the outright gift to Felix Neck Wildlife Sanctuary in December 1979 of an undeveloped tract of land, approximately 85 acres in size, which existed in its natural condition. It abutted Felix Neck Wild Life Sanctuary which at that time had approximately 250 acres and was administered as a wildlife area by Felix Neck under an agreement with the Massachusetts Audobon Society. Farm Neck's donation significantly enhanced and enlarged the Sanctuary. Felix Neck reported in its March 1980 Newsletter:

"In late December of 1979 a dream came true for all of us at Felix Neck – and Gus now really believes in Santa Claus! At that time, the Farm Neck Associates gave Felix Neck over eighty acres of land on the western side of the sanctuary property, as well as the small islands called Brush Island and Great Island in Sengekontacket Pond.

For many years the directors here have felt that the possibility of intensive development of this land in such close proximity was a potential threat to the peace and security of the Neck. Even before the Farm Neck group came into existence, we tried to dream of ways and means by which we might acquire even a small part of this property.

The fact that we now own all of the land needed for our protection, and a beautiful stretch of shore on Major's Cove, we owe to the Farm Neck Associates, who put in the time and work which made this dream possible for us. On our side we share in the responsibility for the future of this fragile area by taking on conservation easements for other areas of the Farm Neck property."

In December 1979, Farm Neck Associates also granted to Felix Neck Wildlife Trust conservation easements and conservation restrictions on over 260 acres so that the areas of the golf course and surrounding open space could only be used for recreation or farming purposes thus guaranteeing that in perpetuity the scenic beauty of the properties abutting Sengekontacket Pond would retain their natural character.

In reporting the sizable gift to Felix Neck, the January 11, 1980 edition of the *Vineyard Gazette* included the following:

"There are 265 acres encircling the course, reaching down to a mile-and-a-half of beach front, and separating 48 house lots on the plan, preserved as open space for eternity. Included in the 85-acre gift to Felix Neck are two tiny islands off the shore and a covenant which gives five acres of the chunk for Vineyard youth lots to be administered by the Vineyard Open Land Foundation (VOLF).

Instead, the 149 half-acre house lots plotted by Strock Enterprises to abut the Felix Neck Wildlife Sanctuary are eliminated and a buffer, forever wild space created in its place. Gus Ben David, the sanctuary's director said this week the land gift ends years of sleepless nights spent worrying about the sanctuary's future.

'The potential of what could have happened is awesome, and Felix Neck has lived with that potential for a good many years. In reality, this is the finest thing that could have happened to Felix Neck because it ensures the peace and tranquility of the sanctuary for people and the biological integrity for the wildlife. Any development on our border would have been disastrous,' he said.

The directors of Felix Neck accepted the gift at their December 14 meeting. They also accepted responsibility for the 265 acres of open space designed into the full parcel.

The Felix Neck land gift made it possible, Mr. Harff said, to preserve the sanctuary's balance and enable the investors to claim a tax write-off.

'It's part of the way in which the project was sold and is financed,' he said. 'For people in a high tax bracket, it's a benefit. So, while this project isn't 100 per cent altruistic, we've preserved a part of the Island that all of us thought was very special.'

Mr. Sweet added:
'There's no money being made by anybody in this project so, to my mind, it is legitimately a conservation project. For everyone involved, we're at an unbelievable stage because there was so much idealism involved. I think we will have a model project when everything is done.'"

Next Farm Neck initiated a significant effort to help the Island's only hospital. In 1986, the first Martha's Vineyard Hospital Tournament was held at Farm Neck and presaged several hospital benefit events held each summer since then. The first tournament was a Pro-Am that attracted ten leading PGA tour professionals and ten club pros from the Cape and Vineyard. The ten pros included Hale Irwin, Curtis Strange, Brad Faxon, Chip Beck, Kenny Knox, Tom Byrum and Miller Barber. Hale Irwin with a 68 led the pros, with only two others breaking par. Sankaty Head's pro had the local pro low score of 74, while Doug DeBettencourt, Farm Neck's host pro, turned in a 77. In an article of September 9, 1986, the Cape Cod Times reported extensively on the first Hospital Pro-Am Golf Tournament. The article included the following comments by Hale Irwin:

"'This is a really fine golf course,' said the two-time U.S. Open Champ after a round that featured four birdies and one bogey. 'It's nice to come out to a course that was designed to be played by everyone, not just tour professionals.'

Irwin was not the only professional to be impressed with the layout. Miller Barber, a member of the Senior PGA Tour, also liked what he saw.

'I was very impressed with the golf course and the tournament in general,' he said. 'Nowadays the courses are designed for knock 'em, sock 'em golf. It was nice to play a course like this where you had to rely on some finesse and all the clubs in your bag.'"

In 1987 members of the PGA Senior Tour were featured among the players in the Hospital Tournament. They included recognized stars such as Tommy Aaron, Miller Barber, Orville Moody and Doug Sanders. The low pro round was a 69 by Bobby Nichols. Once again, the format was a scramble where teams had a touring pro for nine holes and a Vineyard or Cape Cod pro for the other nine holes.

In 1988 Don Bies had the low pro round of 71, besting other touring pros including Harold Henning, Betsy King, Don Massenagle, Orville Moody, Bobby Nichols, Doug Sanders and Bob Toski among others. As was the custom at each of the Hospital Tournaments, during a reception and awards ceremony several of the professionals put on an exhibition, complete with tips for improving participants' golf. Betsy King, the first woman touring pro invited to participate in the Farm Neck Hospital Tournament, made a memorable comment while conducting part of the clinic. She said, "At a recent tournament one of the golfers came into the locker room smiling. When asked why she was so happy she replied, 'I got a new set of golf clubs for my husband,' to which one of the pros replied 'Great trade!'" Her story was particularly appreciated by a number of the ladies present.

In 1989 the low pro round of 68 was shot by Billy Andrade, with Orville Moody not far behind. The following year, the last year in which touring pros were invited to participate in the Hospital Tournament, Brad Faxon led with a 67.

While the presence of the touring pros from the regular, senior and women's tours brought a lot of excitement and interest to the Hospital Tournament, it also became increasingly clear that the net proceeds to the Hospital were significantly lower than the participating supporters hoped, for the escalating costs of bringing in ranking tour players made too large a dent in the gross receipts. Sadly, the period of bringing PGA tour players to Farm Neck came to an end.

For a year or two thereafter, the Tournament continued with participation of club pros from the Vineyard and Cape Cod. In response to participants' suggestions, the format was changed once again. Since 1992 the Farm Neck Hospital Tournament has featured a five-person team scramble, with no professionals invited, so that substantially all the gross proceeds of the annual tournament benefit the Martha's Vineyard Hospital.

After initiating its Annual Hospital Benefit Tournament, Farm Neck undertook a further step in enhancing its contributions to the Vineyard community. In 1989, incident to celebrating Farm Neck's 10th anniversary, the Club announced the establishment of the Farm Neck Foundation. In the annual member booklet, Bob Fullem noted:

"The Farm Neck Foundation is being created to expand upon a tradition at Farm Neck of charity functions to benefit the Island community. From its inception, Farm Neck's original design and guiding principles have been dedicated to creating a very unique place, sensitive to both the land and the community. The Directors believe that this Foundation is an excellent way to carry on those original ideals...Farm Neck will make a matching contribution to the Foundation, from public green fees collected, equal to the members' contribution."

In its very first year, Farm Neck contributed $15,000 to a variety of Island community programs. As Mike Zoll, the first President of the Foundation (and later to become Farm Neck's head pro), reported in 1990, "The response of our membership to the establishment of the Farm Neck Foundation, Inc., was a heartwarming testimony to the concern our members have for the Vineyard community." By 2003 the annual funding of Island needs grew to $41,800. Over the 15 years since the Foundation was established, Farm Neck has made grants totaling $435,272 to 86 Vineyard organizations, ranging across a wide gamut from ones meeting the needs of young children, youths and the elderly, health maintenance and service organizations, environment and resource preservation agencies, cultural organizations, and schools and other educational agencies and facilities. As was noted in the 1995 members' booklet, the Foundation provides:

"...assistance to the many important non-profit agencies on the Island. These agencies play an integral part in preserving and protecting the quality of life on the Vineyard that we all enjoy and, unfortunately, sometimes take for granted. There is not a facet of Island life, from conservation to health care (and everything in between) that is not enhanced by the work of these volunteer groups. Although there is no shortage of dedication and vision within these organizations, there are never enough funds to match...that is where we come in."

In the 1999 member booklet, Tim Sweet's report, as president of the Foundation, stated:

"As gratifying as the last 20 years have been, I can think of no single accomplishment that is a better reflection of who we are and what we believe in, than the establishing of the Farm Neck Foundation...it isn't however the amount of money that gives us the greatest sense of pride, it is the collective willingness of everyone associated with Farm Neck to pitch in and help when asked. Our very unique combination of year-rounders, seasonal and daily visitors, retirees, working stiffs and everyone in between, all sharing the responsibility of giving back to the Island community – that is what has been a pleasure to behold.

For those of us who still find Martha's Vineyard a place like no other, working together to help preserve, protect and promote what brought us here in the first place is not so much charity as just common sense."

In the 2002 Foundation report, Tim noted:

"The sole purpose of our Foundation is to act as a conduit for the public spirit of everyone at Farm Neck. We are indeed fortunate to have so many who recognize our obligation to speak up for and offer support to those in need. Because of the open-handedness of everyone at Farm Neck, we have been able to assist the many wonderful organizations and volunteers working in our behalf to help those in need and preserve the best of Martha's Vineyard."

For a number of years, Farm Neck has also made its facilities available for other community charitable events; for example, a number of the Martha's Vineyard Hospice fundraiser events have been held in the Farm Neck tent, replete with auctions, cocktails and dinner. Similarly, several other Martha's Vineyard Hospital fundraising events were held at Farm Neck, including one in 2000 when President Clinton addressed the audience with insightful comments focused particularly on the challenges of rural health care and one in 2001 when the world-renowned Irish tenor, Ronan Tynan, held the audience spellbound notwithstanding the inclement weather that forced everyone into the Cafe. A golf tournament at Farm Neck has for a number of years benefited Felix Neck and a golf tournament has also been included for a number of years as part of the John Havlicek Celebrity Fishing Tournament, held annually since 1981 to benefit The Genesis Fund that raises money towards the care and treatment of children born with genetic diseases and mental retardation. An annual tennis tournament, including established leading professionals in pro-am events, was initiated several years ago to benefit Time for Life, a foundation providing vacations on the Island for young cancer patients and their families.

Hay rake off the 17th fairway, one of several farm implements left on Farm Neck to recall the property's agricultural heritage.

Eight: *A FINAL THOUGHT*

A s a final thought about the beginnings and history of Farm Neck, nothing captures its spirit better than what Doug Mabee jotted down soon after the Farm Neck project was completed. Among his recollections he noted:

"The story of 'Farm Neck' on Martha's Vineyard, is unique, quixotic, and quite improbable. If we had not been so naïve, we probably never would have attempted such a project — certainly not one based so altruistically on the premise of 'no self-interest or personal gain.' The final result — one of the more meaningful, satisfying events of my lifetime."

Sadly, Doug died in March 2004 and could not join in celebrating our 25th anniversary or have a chance to reminisce by reading this account of a venture to which he contributed wholeheartedly. As was noted in his obituary, *"He was most proud of his involvement as one of three general partners in the founding of Farm Neck Association and Farm Neck Golf Club, Martha's Vineyard, organized to protect 600 acres from real estate development."* Bob Fullem and I totally share Doug's sentiment.

Doug Mabee (1914-2004)

When Doug moved to Florida in the winter of 1983, he resigned as President of Farm Neck. Since then, Bob and I have alternately served as either Chairman of Farm Neck's Board or President. Doug,

View of the 18th hole signage at the tee.

THE
EIGHTEENTH

PAR 5

552
52
488
435

Bob and I, plus Phil Brown and John Williams McGrath constituted the Board for the first five years. Subsequently Tim Sweet was added and Louis Fusari, Don McGrath and Taylor Culbert also served as Directors. For the last several years the Board has been comprised of Gemma Sullivan, Brad Griffith, Luke McGuiness, Bob, Tim and I.

While the Board has had an important role in the development of Farm Neck, the major credit deservedly goes to Tim Sweet and the dedicated staff he has so ably led. Tim's total commitment to quality and esthetics are seen in virtually all aspects of Farm Neck. Moreover, neither he nor we could have accomplished what has been created without the dedication of so many of our long-time staff whose pride in Farm Neck has been so evident in their work. While so many others doubtless deserve to be recognized by name,

thanks particularly is due to a few who have been with Farm Neck most if not all of its first 25 years: Mike Alwardt, our golf course superintendent; John Halenko, the assistant superintendent who first served ably in the pro shop; Fred Sonnenberg, our Club engineer, whose "retirement on the Vineyard" years have kept our equipment and irrigation systems in great shape; Tony and Stella Matta, without whom the Café would not have become so vital a part of Farm Neck; Jude Tucker, our office manager without whom Tim could not have accomplished so much; and Mike Zoll, our head golf pro who has set an exemplary tone for the Club and provided outstanding leadership to our highly competent and dedicated professional teaching and pro shop staff.

Bob's and my letter in the 25th Anniversary Members' booklet sums up well Farm Neck's first quarter century:

View of the 14th hole fairway and green, with Sengekontacket Pond.

———————————————

"There is a lot to be said for being optimistic and farsighted — some thought 'naïve might be more descriptive — about the extent of the challenges before taking on a new venture. Clearly had we fully recognized all the impediments that would face us as we tried to save the beautiful property that now is Farm Neck, we might not have begun on our greatest adventures. In many ways Farm Neck is a shining example of idealism prevailing over realism. Our hope of 25 years ago was simple enough, 'Try to save a pristine corner of Martha's Vineyard from over-development; create a championship caliber golf course for all to enjoy and forever be good stewards of the land.' The execution of that vision, however, was not quite so simple.

First, there was the bank that needed to be persuaded that $1.5 million dollars was a realistic price to relinquish its hold on over 500 acres of waterfront property. Then we needed to persuade 48 investors that $1.5 million was not only not too much to pay for the property, but that we thought we should give away 85 acres of the property to Felix Neck to keep it forever wild. After that, we needed to persuade the Island regulatory agencies that our plan was economically viable and environmentally sound. Next, we had to persuade Oak Bluffs that giving away the development rights on over 265 acres made good fiscal sense for the Town. And finally, we had to find and then persuade the very few golfers on Martha's Vineyard at that time that we were committed to creating a championship caliber golf course and they should consider joining us.

L. Robert Fullem

Simply put, there was not a mad rush by any of the above to embrace our vision. Our needed patrons thought the costs were way too high, the bank thought our offer was way too low, the Town thought the plan would jeopardize its tax base, the permitting agencies weren't sure what to think, and most of the Vineyard's few golfers were sure that we were going to fall on our face. But slowly, with the benefit of some good luck, some good timing and the talent and persuasiveness of some very dedicated people, Farm Neck evolved from a dream to a reality. That evolution continues to this day.

Twenty five years later, Farm Neck remains a work in progress. As rewarding as it was to get Farm Neck off the ground, our greatest source of pride has been watching it grow and mature through all these years. We know of no other golf course anywhere that has undergone our Club's constant and continual renovation, restructuring, restoration and refurbishment. Neither do we know of any other Club that has done so much without member assessments or debt incurrence. Fortunately, our patient willingness to make changes only as the Club could afford them has been richly rewarded as we have watched Farm Neck slowly get better and better each and every year. Since 1979 there has not been a single year that we have not made significant improvements. All told, we have renovated or totally rebuilt every single golf hole on the course, the driving range, the putting greens and the practice and teaching facilities. During the same period, we constructed, expanded or refurbished every one of the 12 buildings on the property, added or enlarged 4 ponds and renovated the entire tennis facility.

Charles H. Harff

129

Twenty-five years ago, our simple hope was to create a first-class, non-exclusive golf setting on the edge of Martha's Vineyard for all to enjoy. But, thanks to a dedicated staff that has been steadfastly committed to the pursuit or excellence, a membership that has been extraordinarily supportive of our goal to be the best we can be, and an ownership that has never lost sight of the original vision, Farm Neck has become far more than we could ever have dreamed. Today Farm Neck stands as one of the most respected golf courses in the Northeast – admired as a true test of golf in an idyllic setting – and welcoming to all those who love the game."

———————————————

Some years ago, I saw a plaque in Sedona, Arizona. Its message is so apt that in closing it is repeated here:

Some men only dream,
Others make dreams
Come true

Tlaquepaque

FARM NECK GOLF CLUB
25th
1979 ~ 2004
MARTHA'S VINEYARD

Footnotes

[1] Island Properties, Inc. v. Martha's Vineyard Commission, 361NE, 2nd 385, at 386.

[2] Massachusetts Statutes 1974, Chapter 737.

[3] In the Matter of Island Properties, Inc. ET AL, Memorandum in Support, Martha's Vineyard Commission File No. 0-128-103, at pages 2 and 14-15.

[4] Decision of the Martha's Vineyard Commission Designating the Oak Bluffs Sengekontacket Pond District as a District of Critical Planning Concern.

[5] House Bill No. 4537.

[6] "The Golf Course of the Future: Economic Realities" published in Urban Land, December 1975.

[7] "The Golf Course of the Future: Economic Realities" published in Urban Land, December 1975.

[8] By 1998/2000 house sites in Farm Neck, very few of which were available for resale, commanded prices in the $850,000 to $925,000 range.

Acknowledgements

Photographs (other than aerials) by Marion MacAfee Harff.

Publication and promotion by Creating Results.

Book layout and cover design by Michael Stakem.